Wonderful *Provençal Cuisine*

Christian Etienne

Photographs:
Didier Benaouda
Translation:
Angela Moyon

Restaurant Christian Etienne
10, rue de Mons
Avignon

ÉDITIONS OUEST-FRANCE
13, rue du Breil - Rennes

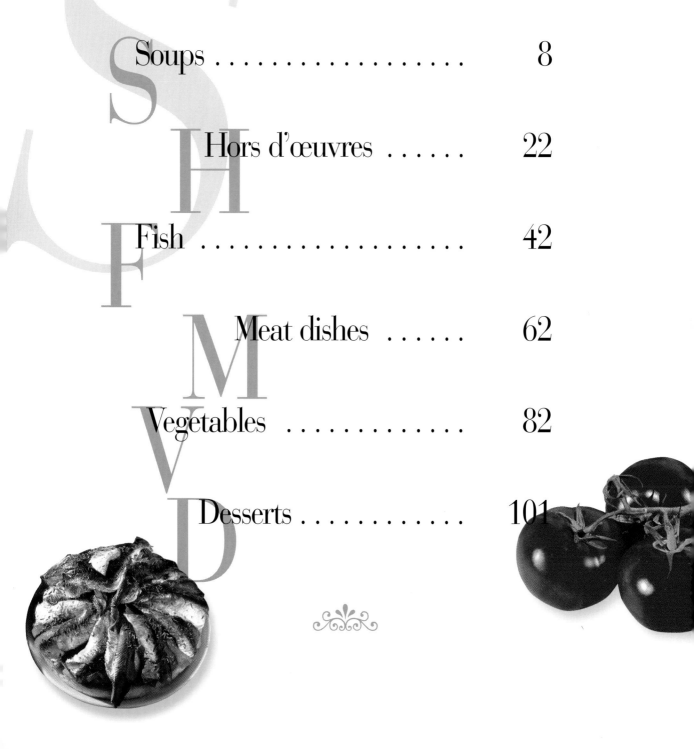

Summary

1 Introduction

Good, high-class cuisine is steeped in character, a local accent and a sense of friendship. Christian Etienne has plenty of character, a pronounced accent and, as far as friendship is concerned, there is plenty to share! His character comes from Provence, his accent is Provençal, and his friendship is both proverbial and Mediterranean.

Provence is an austere but highly-scented region, a region that is unforgettable. When Christian worked at the Intercontinental, he was on the staff with Gagnaire (if you please!). They talked about lambs, the herbs growing on the hillsides, red mullet and dace, olive oil, tender young vegetables and other light, mouthwatering, sun-soaked products that are only to be found south of Montélimar.

Christian retained his nostalgia amid the rush and bustle of the great

Ph. Eric Cattin

hotel and he learned a lot! Anybody with in-bred skill always finds something to learn. Then Christian returned home, to the region of his birth, an area full of tomatoes and truffles, warmed by the sun, swept by the great mistral wind that clears the air, the mind and the heart. Christian came home, determined to pay homage to the land of Provence and the women who gave him his vocation - his two grandmothers and his mother who delighted the family with everything that the gardens and

orchards had to offer, backed up by plenty of family love. Christian has brought two additional touches to this typical Provençal cuisine - the skills of top-class cuisine as practised by one of the finalists in the competition to find the Best Chef in France and his own personal touch, his touch of class!

In this book, he guides you through Provençal cuisine with its stuffed vegetables, braised dishes and some outstanding culinary experiences. He does so in a kindly, discreet manner for true men of Provence are both kind and retiring.

You will find out exactly what makes a good ratatouille and a subtle fisherman's pie. You will discover how ordinary chick peas can be raised to sublime heights by olive oil. You will learn how to make fennel sorbet and pine-kernel tart. When you serve stuffed Provençal mullet to your friends, you will be wearing a chef's hat, handed down by a great chef famous for his kindness and friendliness... Gradually you too will acquire the accent, discover the Camargue and scrub, learn about Provence through the subtlest of its features - its flavours and its aromas!

So it's off to the stove, stew pans and cooking pots and - *bon appétit*!

Robert Ledrole

Soups

Pumpkin Soup

This soup is fairly mild. It is often served in winter. There are several ways of finishing it off but the basic preparation is always the same. I will give you a few variations that we use in Provence.

CREAM OF PUMPKIN SOUP

Serves 10

3 KG PUMPKIN
2 LEEKS (WHITE PARTS ONLY)
3 CLOVES GARLIC
80 G BUTTER
1 LITRE SINGLE CREAM
50 CL MILK
SALT, PEPPER, OLIVE OIL, NUTMEG

• Peel and roughly dice pumpkin. Finely dice leeks and sweat in butter in a large sauté pan. Do not allow to colour.

• Add diced pumpkin and cloves of garlic. Stir over a low heat for 20 to 25 minutes then pour in milk and single cream. Continue to cook, stirring all the time.

• The pumpkin should break down in the sauté pan and become smooth. Strain through a Chinese sieve. Season to taste with salt, pepper and nutmeg.

• Flavour with a few drops of olive oil.

• The Pumpkin Soup is ready to serve.

CREAM OF PUMPKIN WITH TRUFFLES

• 1 litre cream of pumpkin soup + 50 g chopped truffles and a few drops olive oil. Truffles are always added at the last minute to a hot soup.

CREAM OF PUMPKIN WITH PISTOU

• Prepare a «pistou» with 20 g fresh chopped basil, 3 cloves garlic pounded with pestle and mortar and 3 spoons olive oil. Blend the «pistou» into the cream of pumpkin soup.

You can let your imagination run wild with this soup. Cooking is rather like music. One you've learnt the basics, you can be guided by your own inherent good taste.

Cream of Pumpkin with Chives

CREAM OF PUMPKIN WITH CHIVES

•1 litre cream of pumpkin soup + 50 g finely chopped chives blended in at the
last minute.

Tomato and Basil Soup

Serves 6

4 CARROTS
3 ONIONS
1 STICK CELERY
2 WHOLE GARLIC
THYME, BAY
SALT, PEPPER
3 KG TOMATOES
2 DSP. TOMATO PUREE
1 LITRE STOCK
2 SPOONS FLOUR

•Finely dice carrots, onions, and celery and chop the garlic. Sweat in olive oil. Cut 2 kg tomatoes into rough cubes and cook slowly over a low heat as if making a sauce. Peel and remove seeds from remaining 1 kg tomatoes. Liquidise flesh and stir into soup. Season to taste. Serve chilled with chopped basil.

•This soup can also be served hot - and with the addition of a drop or two of olive oil, it's not bad at all.

Fish Soup

This soup takes some time to prepare but it is so delicious that it is worth the time and effort! Your fishmonger will have a range of small fish that are ideal for this recipe.

Ingredients

3 KG RED SOUP
1 LEEK
1 FENNEL
3 WHOLE GARLIC (HALVED)
1 ONION
250 G TOMATO PUREE
2 G SAFFRON
THYME, BAY

There are several types of fish soup - «grey» or «trawler» soup which is much less expensive but not very tasty, and «red» or «rock» soup made with small red fish which is excellent.

Fish Soup

• Sweat all the vegetables without allowing them to colour. Add fish (red soup), tomato puree, and saffron. Stir well until fish begins to break up. Add water to cover. Cook for 2 hours, with a slow rolling boil. Strain through a Chinese sieve (the mesh should not be too fine). Check seasoning (salt, pepper) and keep warm. There should be at least 5 litres of stock left. Serve with grilled croutons and some rouille (mayonnaise flavoured with garlic and pimento).

• Some people add grated Swiss cheese but personally I prefer this soup without.

For 2 litres soup

2 KG CRAB
2 CARROTS
2 SHALLOTS
3 CLOVES GARLIC
2 LEEKS (WHITE PART ONLY, FOR GARNISH)
1 STICK CELERY
THYME, BAY
3 DSP TOMATO PUREE
OLIVE OIL, SALT, PEPPER
1 RED PIMENTO
50 CL WHITE WINE

CRAB AND LEEK SOUP

This soup is usually made with small brown sand crabs but green crabs can also be used. The most important thing is that they should be alive.

• Roughly dice carrots, quarter shallots and crush garlic.

• Heat olive oil in a fairly large stew pan. When oil is smoking, add crabs and shake pan continuously. The crabs should be red on all sides.

• Add vegetables and sweat for a few minutes then add tomato puree and quickly pour in white wine.

• Barely cover with water, season with salt and pepper, then add red pimento. Cook for 20 minutes.

• Strain through wide-meshed sieve, crushing the crabs well, then strain again through a fine-meshed Chinese sieve. Put back on heat for 15 to 20 minutes to bring out full flavour.

• The soup should be deep red in colour and have a good, strong flavour.

Try fried leeks as an easy, amusing garnish. They add a pleasant, crisp finish.

• Cut the white parts of the leek in sections 15 cm (6 ins.) long. Split in two and chop finely to make a julienne.

• Bring frying oil up to 150°C and add leeks, a few at a time. When golden brown, remove with a vegetable strainer and immediately season with salt.

• Sprinkle a few leek "chips" in the soup plates before serving.

• Try this soup with a glass of white Lirac for a really enjoyable experience.

• The soup can also be served with well-boiled pudding rice or thick vermicelli.

Cream of Lentil Soup

CREAM OF LENTIL SOUP

We use green lentils from Le Puy for this soup, as preferred by my friend, Régis Marcon, one of the region's great chefs.

In Provence, lentils were traditionally cooked with a piece of salt pork in a large quantity of water. The cooking liquor was served as a clear soup with dry bread and the lentils were eaten either as a salad or warm with the salt pork. With a main course to follow, there was enough for the week.

Here, I am giving you the recipe used in my restaurant in the winter months.

• Sweat diced pork in olive oil. Once it is golden brown, add lentils, pour over water and add vegetables. Cook for an hour, remove vegetables and mash. Check and correct seasoning. Add a few drops of olive oil.

• Just before serving, add whipped cream and blend well in a liquidiser.

• This soup can also be eaten cold. It has a very subtle taste and, with the addition of well-flavoured olive oil, it is absolutely delicious.

Serves 10

300 G GREEN LENTILS
1 CARROT
1 ONION
2 CLOVES GARLIC
100G SALT PORK (ROUGHLY DICED)
2.5 LITRES WATER
25 CL WHIPPED CREAM
OLIVE OIL

SPELT SOUP

Spelt is a sort of wild corn which grows in the mountains of Provence, on the Sault Plateau and in the Ventoux area. It is a rustic plant, which makes it very tasty. It can be bought under the name of "small spelt", the best kind. The following is a very old recipe which is worth making for curiosity's sake. However, it has to be said that this is a soup for country folk; few city dwellers eat it because it is rather filling.

• Place leg of mutton in a stew pan, knuckle end underneath. Pour in 3 litres water and bring to boil, skimming occasionally to remove any impurities that float up to the surface.

• Add onion, garlic, celery, carrots, bay leaf and thyme. Salt lightly and simmer for 2 hours. Top up with water to maintain the quantity at 3 litres.

• Strain stock and set aside meat and vegetables which constitute a separate course.

• Place 300 g spelt in a large stew pan and pour on stock. Simmer for 30 to 45 minutes. Check seasoning and serve soup as it is, with a few drops of olive oil.

• This may be rustic but it is also very tasty.

• For a more sophisticated result, mash with a potato masher. The individual grains of spelt are no longer visible and the soup is more elegant. If it is too thick, add some water.

Ingredients

300 G SPELT
1 KG LEG OF MUTTON
1 ONION STUDDED WITH CLOVES
1 CLOVE GARLIC
1 STICK CELERY
2 CARROTS
1 BAY LEAF
1 SPRIG THYME
SALT, PEPPER, OLIVE OIL

Spelt and Sausage Soup

In winter, I often make Spelt and Sausage Soup. Here is the recipe:

Serves 10

4 SAUSAGES
300G SMALL SPELT
1 STICK CELERY, THYME AND BAY FOR A BOUQUET
GARNI
1 CARROT
1 ONION STUDDED WITH 4 CLOVES

• Cook sausages in 3.5 litres water with vegetables and bouquet garni for 1 to 1 1/2 hours depending on size.

• Pour stock over spelt and cook for 30 to 40 minutes.

• Meanwhile, when sausages are cold, cut into thick slices (2 to 3 cm, approx. 1 in.) and grill. Add sliced sausages to soup as garnish.

• This is a good, tasty winter soup which can be washed down with a glass of red wine (a Gigondas is a good choice).

Vegetable and Herb Soup

Serves 10

1 ONION
5 CARROTS
3 TURNIPS
6 STICKS GOOD WHITE CELERY
2 FRESH TOMATOES (SKINNED AND ROUGHLY DICED)
3 POTATOES (KING EDWARD TYPE)
3 COURGETTES
1 BAY LEAF, 1 SPRIG THYME, 10G CHOPPED CHIVES, 1 CLOVE GARLIC

Soup is always enjoyable in winter and there is no end of choice, whether eaten hot or cold. This is a recipe for a very good clear soup because, as the vegetables are chopped, they retain their taste and texture, set off by the aromas and flavours of the stock.

• Make a clear stock with 1 roughly-chopped carrot, 1 turnip, 1 courgette, 1 onion and all the celery leaves.

• Sweat finely-chopped onion and add vegetables, clove of garlic, thyme and bay. Add enough water to cover. Season lightly with salt and simmer.

• Meanwhile, finely chop remainder of vegetables. Cut carrots, turnips and courgettes in four lengthways and chop finely. Peel celery and chop finely.

• Cook vegetables separately in a small quantity of stock in a different pan.

• Cook al dente and immediately cool in iced water to stop the cooking process.

• Then place in a soup tureen. Add diced, uncooked tomato, chopped chives and some olive oil. Just before serving, pour hot stock over vegetables.

Vegetable and Herb Soup

ROUILLE

Ingredients

2 CLOVES GARLIC
1/4 RED PIMENTO
1 SLICE BREAD SOAKED IN MILK
OLIVE OIL

- Pound all ingredients with a pestle and mortar or blend in a liquidiser.
- Add 20 cl olive oil to make a paste.
- Add 20 cl mussel soup.
- Rouille can also be served with fish soup, in which case the paste is blended with fish soup.

Pistou Soup

Pistou Soup

- Top, tail and string green beans and cut into pieces.
- Dice courgettes.
- Cook green beans in 2.5 litres water with salt and pepper. After 15 minutes, add carrots and potatoes. After a further 15 minutes add courgettes.
- Cook for 15 minutes then add vermicelli.
- Crush tomato flesh, peeled garlic, parmesan and basil leaves, gradually dribbling on olive oil.
- Pour into boiling soup.

This soup originated in Genoa. It is now served piping hot in the autumn and cold in the summer. It can be made more or less refreshing depending on the quantity of tomatoes used. We often add a few bacon rinds which are beginning to turn rancid.

This is a typical Provençal summer dish.

Ingredients

100 G LARGE GREEN BEANS
100 G WHITE HARICOT BEANS
2 OR 3 COURGETTES
100 G CARROTS
50 G POTATOES
100 G LARGE VERMICELLI
4 VERY RIPE TOMATOES
5 CLOVES GARLIC
1 BUNCH BASIL
75 G PARMESAN CHEESE
25 CL OLIVE OIL
2.5 LITRES WATER

Snail and Mild Garlic Soup

- If the garlic is old, remove sprouts and use 120g.
Heat puree.
- Blanch garlic three times to remove all trace of bitterness. To do so, place cloves in a small saucepan, cover with cold milk and bring to boil. Remove from heat as soon as milk boils, drain garlic and throw away milk. Repeat this procedure twice more.
- Drain snails. If you are using wild snails, leave to disgorge then cook with a few cloves garlic and a large sprig of fennel. Drain.
- Heat snails in a frying pan with olive oil, add well-dried garlic and carefully shop. Season with salt and pepper.
- Roughly cut up parsley and sprinkle over snails. Stir once or twice. Place mixture in a soup tureen.
- Add tomato flesh to boiling puree. Then pour into soup tureen and stir carefully before serving.

Serves 4

1 LITRE TOMATO PUREE
200 G TOMATOES (FLESH ONLY)
100 G CLOVES GARLIC (PEELED)
100 G FLAT PARSLEY
24 OR 48 TINNED SNAILS (QUANTITY DEPENDS ON PERSONAL PREFERENCE)
MILK
SALT, PEPPER

CREAM OF CHICKEN AND FROG SOUP

Serves 6

1 LITRE STOCK
80 G FLOUR
80 G BUTTER
SALT, PEPPER
LEMON, NUTMEG
50 CL FRESH CREAM
18 FROGS' LEGS
50 CL MILK

- Begin by making the white sauce. To do so, make a roux with 80g butter and 80g flour. Pour in stock and cook for at least 1hr over a low heat. Long, slow cooking completely removes the taste of the flour.
- Meanwhile, poach frogs' legs in milk.
- Bring to boil then drain and dry. Carefully bone frogs' legs and place meat in the soup tureen. Cover with a lid and stir from time to time.
- At the end of the cooking time, blend cream into the white sauce, whipping firmly but slowly.
- Put back on the heat to finish off. The soup should be smooth and white.
- Check seasoning, add juice of half a lemon, and grate in a small quantity of nutmeg.
- Stir, remove from heat and pour hot cream soup over frogs' leg.

OYSTER SOUP

Serves 6

18 BOUZIGUES OR VERTES DE CLAIRE OYSTERS
80 G BUTTER
100 G FLOUR
1 LITRE WELL-FLAVOURED CHICKEN STOCK
1/2 LEMON (JUICE ONLY)
SALT, PEPPER

- Open oysters, strain juice and set aside.
- Make a cream sauce. Prepare a roux by melting butter, adding flour and stirring briefly. To ensure that roux stays white, avoid overcooking flour on an excessively high heat. Cool roux then pour on stock; this method avoids the formation of lumps.
- Whip, place back on the heat for 30 minutes. Strain then check consistency, adding stock and reducing down again. The soup should resemble single cream.
- Do not add salt. Season with pepper and nutmeg.
- Add juice from oysters and put back on heat with lemon juice.
- Lay oysters out in each plate then pour on boiling soup which will seal in their flavour without overcooking.

MUSSEL AND SAFFRON SOUP

Serves 10

4 KG MUSSELS
50 CL WHITE WINE
2 CARROTS (FINELY CHOPPED)
1 ONION (FINELY CHOPPED)
2 CLOVES GARLIC (FINELY CHOPPED)
1 TOMATO
1 G SAFFRON
PEPPER, THYME, BAY, OLIVE OIL

We often use mussels from the Etang de Tau but the soup can also be made with mussels grown on stakes, which are smaller but sometimes fuller.

- Wash mussels well. Steam open in white wine with thyme and bay but do not overcook or mussels will be rubbery and dry.
- Remove from shells and set aside in a soup tureen.

•Strain cooking liquor ensuring that there is no sand left (it often drops to the bottom of the saucepan).

•Heat olive oil in another pan, add carrots and onions. When golden, add garlic then tomato and saffron.

•Taste mussel cooking liquor to ensure that it is not too salty before pouring over vegetables. If it is too salty, add water.

•Bring to boil and pour very hot liquor over mussels.

•Serve with grilled croutons rubbed with garlic or with rouille.

Mussel and Saffron Soup

SNAIL AND WHITE-BEET SOUP

Serves 10

5 WHITE-BEET, WITH LEAVES
60 SNAILS
3 LITRES WELL-FLAVOURED CHICKEN STOCK
OLIVE OIL
SALT, PEPPER, FRESH HERBS, PARSLEY, CHIVES

This soup is almost a meal in itself. We use "petits-gris", small tasty snails which feed on the herbs that grow wild in Provence - thyme, fennel etc.

I advise you to buy tinned snails because the preparation of fresh snails takes a long time and the result is not always any better than you will get with the canned product.

- Prepare white-beet, keeping green leaves as large as possible. Blanch leaves in salted water for 5 minutes then plunge into ice to retain colour.

Snail and White-Beet Soup

- Peel stalks and cut into small sticks 2cm (1 in.) long and 0.5 cm (1/4 in.) wide.
- Again cook in salted water and plunge into ice.

Wash snails well. Prepare a well-flavoured chicken stock.

- Blend white-beet stalks with snails, fines herbes and a few spoons olive oil.
- Line soup tureen with white-beet leaves. Heat white-beet and snails slightly. Place in soup tureen and pour on very hot chicken stock after checking seasoning.

This recipe was given to me by my nephew, Cyril, who helps me in the kitchen and I have to say that it is excellent.

CREAM OF ASPARAGUS SOUP

•If you have whole asparagus left, or the ends of asparagus after cutting the tips, it is a pity to throw away the rather hard stem. Here is a recipe for a cream soup that will tickle your tastebuds.

•Melt butter with finely chopped onions. Add finely-diced asparagus stalks (set aside tips if you have any).

•Add flour as if making a roux. Cook for a few minutes, stirring continuously, then pour on chicken stock as if making a bechamel. Simmer gently for 1 hour. The soup should not be too thick.

•Strain through a fine-meshed Chinese sieve and check seasoning. Add nutmeg and lemon juice. At the last minute, add single cream and bring to boil.

•If you prefer a lighter soup, blend in a liquidiser before serving.

Serves 8 to 10

1 KG WELL PEELED ASPARAGUS
1 LITRE CHICKEN STOCK
2 LARGE ONIONS
50 CL WHIPPED SINGLE CREAM
100 G BUTTER
80 G FLOUR
1 LEMON (JUICE ONLY)
SALT, PEPPER, NUTMEG

CREAM OF CELERY SOUP

•Finely chop white parts of leeks and sweat slowly in olive oil in a saucepan.

•Finely dice celeriac, add to leeks and pour on 1/2 litre of veal stock and an equal quantity of water.

•Leave soup to cook. Meanwhile, fry tiny croutons of bread in butter. The croutons give the soup a "bit of bite".

•When the celeriac is cooked, blend as for a vegetable soup preferably in a Moulinette (a liquidiser puts too much air into the vegetables and changes the taste).

•Check seasoning and pour over small croutons.

The celeriac should soften the hearts of your guests!

Serves 6

1 KG LEEKS (WHITE PARTS ONLY)
1 KG CELERIAC
50 CL VEAL STOCK
SLICED BREAD
BUTTER, OLIVE OIL
SALT, PEPPER

OXTAIL, CELERY AND TRUFFLE SOUP

•Prepare oxtail and make stock, cooking it like a stew with the usual herbs and flavourings, onion studded with cloves, bouquet garni, black pepper corns, and stew vegetables drained, sliced and blended into the ones in the herbs and flavourings.

•Meanwhile, finely dice carrot and celery. Sauté vegetables for 5 minutes in olive oil. Preheat oven (mark 8).

•Place diced truffles in a soup tureen with vegetables, well-flavoured stock and meat, cover with a thin layer of puff pastry.

•Serve when the pastry is cooked. As soon as you remove the pastry "lid" the powerful aroma of this soup will waft round the room.

Serves 4

1 GOOD-SIZED OXTAIL
300 G TRUFFLES
1 CARROT
100 G GOOD WHITE CELERY
PUFF PASTRY
SALT, PEPPER
1 BOUQUET GARNI (AS USED FOR BEEF STEW)

Hors d'œuvres

HERB AND TOMATO TARTAR WITH RAW SHALLOT

Serves 6

10 LARGE TOMATOES
1 SHALLOT
1 BUNCH OF BASIL
OLIVE OIL FROM MAUSSANE
SALT, PEPPER

- Skin tomatoes, slice, remove seeds and roughly chop flesh.
- Press for as long as possible.
- Moisten with olive oil.

**Herb and Tomato Tartar
with Raw Shallot**

- Season with salt and pepper. Add chopped basil and sliced shallot.
- Place in round moulds to serve, dribbling olive oil over at the last minute.

Serves 6 to 8

250 G COOKED CHICK PEAS IN BRINE
2 TO 3 CLOVES GARLIC (CRUSHED)
2 LEMONS (JUICE ONLY)
1 DSP. OLIVE OIL
1 PINCH PAPRIKA
SALT
PIMENTO TO TASTE
1 DSP. CHOPPED PARSLEY
CHICKEN STOCK

PROVENÇAL HUMUS

- Put chick peas through a vegetable mixer than liquidise with lemon juice, crushed garlic, seasoning and chicken stock to obtain a puree that is not too thick.
- Heat over a low heat.

• Serve in a large bowl, dusted with paprika and chopped parsley.

• Dribble on olive oil and sprinkle with grilled sesame seeds.

This is an aperitif "dip" eaten with slices of toast and a good white wine.

SMALL, TARRAGON-STUFFED TOMATOES

Serves 6

18 SMALL ROUND TOMATOES
2KG MARMANDE TOMATOES
10 TARRAGON LEAVES
25 CL BEEF STOCK
2 CLOVES GARLIC
1 ONION
OLIVE OIL

- Skin small tomatoes and remove seeds. Place upside down to drain.
- Take 2kg Marmande tomatoes: skin, remove seeds, dice.
- Sweat onion and garlic in olive oil with diced tomatoes.
- Reduce down.
- Add chopped tarragon leaves and fill tomatoes.
- Cook for 10 minutes in a hot oven with beef stock and serve as they are.

This is a mouthwatering accompaniment to red meats or oily fish such as mackerel or sardines. On their own, the tomatoes can be eaten hot or cold.

Small, Tarragon-Stuffed Tomatoes

**Anchovies Marinated in
Lemon and Fines Herbes**

ANCHOVIES MARINATED
IN LEMON AND FINES HERBES

•Buy freshly-caught anchovies, lift the filets and place carefully in a dish. Season with salt and pepper and pour over some lemon juice.

•Leave to marinate in the lemon juice for a few minutes then pour over some good olive oil. Add parsley, chervil and chopped chives.

•I do not give any quantities for this recipe because you can prepare as many as you can eat. With a few slices of toasted country loaf, still warm, anchovies are a wonderful aperitif.

Sardines can be prepared in the same way.

Sardine and Tomato Quiche

Sardines

Sardines - mmmm! What superb fish. Sardines are thought to have originated in the Secondary Era, 400 million years ago. And if great chefs of days gone by have never devoted a few chapters to the sardine, we in Provence find this a pity. There are even those among us who claim that this is a delicacy.

Of course, everybody has heard the story of the sardine that blocked the entrance to Marseilles harbour - it was the boat, needless to say, not the fish!

SARDINE AND TOMATO QUICHE

- Line the tin with puff pastry. Bake blind, covering pastry base with dried haricot beans or butter beans to prevent it from rising. Bake through, until golden.
- Meanwhile, fillet sardines. Drain well on a cloth.
- When pastry base is cooked, leave to cool then spread preserved tomatoes over base. Lay out sardines to form a wheel, tails towards the centre.
- Season with salt and pepper, sprinkle with thyme, dribble on olive oil and bake in a hot oven (170 to 180°C) for 10 minutes.

Serves 6

1 CAKE TIN, DIA. 30 CM (12 IN.)
300 G HOME-PRESERVED TOMATOES
500 G FRESH SARDINES
THYME
OLIVE OIL, SALT, PEPPER
300 G PUFF PASTRY

Preserved tomatoes

- Choose long Italian tomatoes for this recipe. They should be red and ripe but not over-ripe. Cut in half, remove seeds and lay out on a baking sheet leaving plenty of space between them.
- Season with salt and pepper, sprinkle on a pinch of sugar, dust with thyme to flavour and add additional flavour with a few cloves of garlic (crushed).
- Pour on some olive oil and leave in the oven for 4 hours at 100°C.
- Put in a cool place for a few days.

- The quiche can be served piping hot with a glass of white Laudan from the Quatre-Chemins cellar. This is Pleasure with a capital "P", at its gastronomic best. However, if you have any quiche left, it is equally mouthwatering served cold.
- Sardines are also excellent when grilled and served with a mustard sauce. We advise you to grill the sardines outside, though, because the smell of grilled sardines is not very pleasant indoors.
- Local fishermen in Provence grill them without gutting them. They merely rinse them under slow running water first. By grilling them, the scales are removed and, although the local people eat only the fillets, the innards add a wonderful taste and aroma.

MACKEREL IN WHITE WINE

Serves 10

10 MACKEREL
2 CARROTS
2 ONIONS
3 SHALLOTS
2 GARLIC CLOVES
1 BOUQUET GARNI (THYME, BAY, PARSLEY AND STICK OF CELERY)
1 LITRE GOOD DRY WHITE WINE
SALT, PEPPER, OLIVE OIL
BALSAMIC VINEGAR

Mackerel is an excellent oily fish but it must be absolutely fresh, with clear shiny eyes and firm flesh. Ignore the appearance of the gills; they are often red in mackerel and cannot be used to judge freshness.

• Finely chop all vegetables and sweat for 10 minutes in olive oil. Pour in white wine, add bouquet garni and simmer for 20 minutes on a gentle heat.

• Meanwhile, fillet mackerel taking care to remove all the bones. Place fillets on the serving dish, season with salt and pepper and pour over a generous amount of olive oil.

Mackerel in White Wine

• When everything is ready, pour the cooked vegetables and white wine over the mackerel. Bring fish and vegetables back to the boil for a few seconds and set out on a serving dish. The dish can be eaten hot or cold. Add a few drops of balsamic vinegar for an excellent, inexpensive hors d'oeuvre for large families.

• Serve with a good white wine.

FISHERMAN'S PIE WITH GARLIC CROUTONS

Ingredients

1 KG SALT COD
1 KG COD
1 LITRE MILK
1 LITRE OLIVE OIL
1 WHOLE GARLIC
1 FRENCH STICK LOAF
150 G TRUFFLES

• On the previous day, soak cod to remove salt. Poach with fresh cod in milk then thicken with olive oil. Drain.

• Using a wooden spoon or spatula, stir vigorously over a very low heat and blend in olive oil until smooth.

• At the last minute, blend in crushed, pureed garlic and finely-sliced truffles. Check seasoning (be careful not to add too much salt).

• Spread on toasted slices of baguette.

"Brandade" is one of the greatest specialities of the town of Nîmes. In days gone by, the people of Nîmes used to trade with fishermen, exchanging fish for salt. They removed the salt from the cod by placing it in the cistern over the toilet.

**Fisherman's Pie
with Garlic Croutons**

White Wine and Rabbit Terrine

Serves 10

1 HOME-BRED RABBIT
2 CARROTS
5 SHALLOTS
1 ONION
3 CLOVES GARLIC
2 ORANGES (ZESTS ONLY)
1 LEMON (ZEST ONLY)
1.5 LITRES WHITE CHÂTEAUNEUF-DU-PAPE WINE
SALT, PEPPER
20 G CHOPPED FLAT PARSLEY
20 G CHOPPED CHIVES
10 G TARRAGON
THYME, BAY LEAF

This is an easy recipe which is quick to make. It can be kept in the larder as a good, cool hors d'oeuvre for unexpected guests.

- Bone rabbit and cut into large pieces.
- Roughly chop carrots, shallot, onion and garlic.
- Finely dice orange and lemon zests.
- Mix all dry ingredients and pour on Châteauneuf-du-Pape. Marinate for 24 hours.
- To make stock with bones: sweat bones in a large saucepan, then cover with water and add thyme and bay. Simmer very gently until almost reduced away.
- The next day, add fines herbes and stock to marinated rabbit. Season with 14 g salt per kilo and 3 g pepper. Place mixture in a terrine and cook for 3 hours in a moderate oven (140 to 160°C).
- Once cooked, leave to cool. Do not serve until the following day.

This is a very well-flavoured rabbit in aspic terrine.

It is delightful served with a few gherkins and pickled onions. It is also very tasty with a few lettuce leaves or peppers marinated in olive oil.

Serves 10

400 G COOKED SPINACH
400 G COOKED WHITE-BEET LEAVES
50 G COOKED SORREL
100 G ONIONS (FINELY CHOPPED AND COOKED)
3 CLOVES GARLIC (CRUSHED)
100 G FATTY BACON (FINELY CHOPPED)
200 G PORK CAUL (WELL RINSED)
THYME, BAY, SAGE
1 LITRE CHICKEN STOCK

Dumplings

Herb dumplings

- Mix all ingredients in a large dish. Season well with salt and pepper.
- Make dumplings weighing approximately 110 g (just under 4 oz.) and roll in caul. Lay out in an ovenproof dish and pour on stock, half covering the dumplings.
- Top with thyme, bay and sage and bake for 2 hours at a low heat (130 to 140°C).

White Wine and Rabbit Terrine

Game dumplings

GAME DUMPLINGS

Serves 10

500 G GAME MEAT (CHEAPER CUTS ARE FINE)
200 G COOKED SPINACH
50 G COOKED SORREL
100 G ONIONS (FINELY CHOPPED AND COOKED)
150 G TO 200G PORK CAUL
5 JUNIPER BERRIES
THYME, BAY, SAGE
1 LITRE STOCK

•Cut game into small piece and cook slowly as if making a stew. This produces a good, dry dumpling.

•Make dumpling with spinach, onion, garlic, thyme and game and crushed juniper berries.

•Make small balls weighing approximately 30 g (just over 1 oz.) and roll in caul.

•Lay out in an ovenproof dish and pour on stock, half covering the dumplings.

•Place sage and bay leaves on top and cook for a good hour at a low heat (140°C).

LAMB DUMPLINGS

•Make in the same way as the game dumpling, replacing game with lamb. Use well-braised pieces of neck, loin or breast.

Dumplings are served hot with the cooking juice remaining in the dish lightly seasoned with a vinaigrette or cold as a morning snack.

Local farmers or wine-growers often take them into the fields for lunch with a red Côtes-du-Rhône. They make a good meal.

PORK CHEESE

Pork cheese was a tradition when a pig was killed in country districts. The event was an excuse for celebrations to which all the neighbours were invited.

This is one of those rather rich but very rustic morning snacks or hors d'oeuvres.

It also has its place on country buffet tables and is a firm favourite with France's current President, Jacques Chirac.

This was my grandparents' recipe.

**Pork Cheese
with Fines Herbes**

Pork Cheese with Fines Herbes

Ingredients

1/2 HEAD OF A PIG, WITH TONGUE
1 KNUCKLE
2 TROTTERS
3 CARROTS
2 ONIONS STUCK WITH 5 CLOVES
2 STICKS GREEN CELERY
1 WHOLE GARLIC (HALVED)
THYME, BAY
40 G BAY
30 G CHIVES
15 G TARRAGON

• Clean head, trotters, knuckle and tongue by soaking for half-a-day in fresh water. Clean head and trotters well and cut or burn off any remaining bristles.

• When all ingredients are clean, place in a large pan. Cover with water, stir well, add salt (14 g cooking salt to 1 litre water) and pepper (3g pepper for 1l water). Cook for 5 hours, skimming regularly to remove any impurities rising to the surface.

• At the end of the 5 hours, allow to cool until the pieces of meat can be removed. Remove all bones and roughly chop meat. Place in a terrine that is big enough to leave room to mix the ingredients. Check seasoning and add fines herbes.

• Fill several terrines or jars with chopped meat and add cooking liquor at the last moment. Mix well to ensure that the stock soaks into all the meat.

• Place terrines in a cold place and leave for 2 or 3 days before eating with good country bread and a good glass of red wine e.g. Château La Nerthe (Châteauneuf-du-Pape).

Young mackerel

Try to find young mackerel under 1 year old. They are caught on the surface and are much less oily than an adult mackerel.

Serves 10

Pressed Mackerel and Fennel

2 KG MACKEREL
2 KG FENNEL
50 CL WHITE WINE
2 CARROTS
2 ONIONS
4 CLOVES GARLIC
1 G SAFFRON
THYME, BAY, OLIVE OIL

•Fillet mackerel. Season with salt and pepper and lay out flat on a baking tray. Oil lightly.

•Bring white wine to the boil and pour over fillets.

Boil fillets for 2 to 3 seconds only. Set aside and leave to cool.

•Meanwhile, cut fennel into six pieces. Blanch in salted water (boil for 4 minutes and always use 14 g salt to 1 litre water). Cool and drain. Finely chop carrots and onions. In a pan big enough to take the fennel, fry onions and carrots until almost ready to colour.

•Add chopped garlic and place fennel over the top. Add saffron, salt and pepper. Pour on white wine used to cook the mackerel and finish off with water so that the fennel is well covered. Cook over a low heat.

•When fennel is cooked, remove from pan and drain.

•Reduce remaining liquor by half. Prepare a terrine, alternating layers of mackerel and fennel. Blend in remaining liquor and put in a cold place overnight.

•The next day, slice using an electric knife and serve cold with a fines herbes vinaigrette.

This recipe goes very well with a white Côtes-du-Rhône wine (Domaine de la Présidente).

**Pressed Mackerel
and Fennel**

Mixed asparagus Salad

Asparagus

• Asparagus is the most outstanding of all spring vegetables. It reaches our tables just after the end of winter, the period during which we eat a lot of game and pork products. In days gone by, people used to say that, with its marked diuretic properties, asparagus arrived to purify the body.

• Whether white, purple or green, this is a very tasty vegetable. The larger the asparagus, the more the taste, but it always has to be eaten very fresh.

• Asparagus usually needs to be peeled, then tied together in a bunch and cooked in well-salted water. Cooking times depend on size.

• Asparagus should always be cooked in plenty of water then plunged into iced water to stop the cooking process and, in the case of green asparagus, ensure it remains green.

• Asparagus is best eaten with a vinaigrette. If too cold, it loses a lot of its taste.

Here is a suggestion for a vinaigrette that provides an excellent accompaniment for asparagus.

VINAIGRETTE

• Blend all the ingredients together and dip the asparagus in the vinaigrette. It's delicious!

Ingredients

1 DSP. BALSAMIC VINEGAR
6 DSP. OLIVE OIL
SALT, PEPPER
15 G CHOPPED CHIVES
2 G CHOPPED TARRAGON
5 G CHOPPED FLAT PARSLEY
10 G PRESERVED TOMATOES

MIXED ASPARAGUS SALAD

• Place mixed green salad in the centre of the plate. Put alternating green and white asparagus on the lettuce to form a dome.

• Dot with preserved tomatoes and black olives and moisten with vinaigrette.

This is a very attractive, and very tasty, hors dœuvre.

Serves 10

30 GREEN ASPARAGUS TIPS
30 WHITE ASPARAGUS TIPS
20 G CHOPPED BLACK OLIVES
PRESERVED TOMATOES
HERB VINEGAR
ENOUGH MIXED GREEN SALAD FOR ALL THE GUESTS

Brains

Brains are a common hors d'oeuvre in Provence. They can also be served as a main course if you are not very hungry.

LAMB'S BRAIN WITH CAPERS

Ingredients

1 OR 2 LAMB'S BRAINS
1 BAY LEAF
FLOUR
BUTTER
OLIVE OIL
30G CAPERS

•If serving as an hors d'oeuvre, allow one brain for two; for a main dish, allow one brain per person.

•Clean for a few hours in fresh water to remove any traces of blood. Poach in salted water containing vinegar and a bay leaf. Bring to boil and leave in water to cool.

•Drain the brain, cut into quarters, dust with flour and fry in a hot pan containing a mixture of one-half butter and one-half olive oil. Fry until golden on all sides and place on a serving dish.

•Remove any fat remaining in frying pan and add lightly chopped capers. Add 50 g butter and fry until golden brown.

•Pour over brains, which should be eaten very hot accompanied by a few lettuce leaves and a light red wine.

BRAIN FRITTERS

•Prepare brains as indicated in the capers recipe but cut into large pieces. Dip in batter and deep fry.

•This is delicious served with tomato sauce.

Batter

125G FLOUR
1 PINCH SALT
2 SPOONS OLIVE OIL
20 CL SLIGHTLY WARM WATER
2 EGG WHITES

Batter

•Mix all ingredients with a wooden spoon and leave for 2 hours. Just before using add 2 stiffly-beaten egg whites.

POULTRY LIVER FLAN

Serves 6 to 8

200 G POULTRY LIVERS
6 EGGS
1 LITRE SINGLE CREAM
SALT, PEPPER, NUTMEG
2 GREY SHALLOTS
1 CLOVE GARLIC

•Liquidise ingredients. Be careful not to overheat and introduce too much air into livers. Turn liquidiser on and off in short bursts. Season with 10 g salt, 3 g pepper, and some grated nutmeg. Pass through a fine-meshed Chinese sieve. The mixture should be moist.

Lamb's brain with Capers

•Lightly grease dariole moulds. Fill with mixture and cook in a bain-marie at Th.6 for 2 hours.

•Cool and store for 3 days in the refrigerator. It takes 3 days to bring out and blend the flavours.

Lamb's Tongue and Brain Salad

POULTRY HEART KEBABS

- Cut hearts in half. Ensure that there is no blood remaining. Remove any traces of arteries or veins.
- Finely slice truffles.
- Marinate hearts with the truffles in good olive oil for approximately 1 hour.
- Place hearts on skewers and cook in a frying pan. Do not barbecue over embers.
- Seal by cooking quickly over a very strong heat and immediately dipping into port wine sauce.

Ingredients

POULTRY HEARTS (3 PER KEBAB)
TRUFFLES
OLIVE OIL
PORT AND TRUFFLE SAUCE

LAMB'S TONGUE AND BRAIN SALAD

A "mesclun" is a mixture of various varieties of young lettuce and herbs. It is made with the lettuces removed when thinning a row.

This salad is almost a meal in itself in the summer or it can provide a family with a copious hors d'oeuvre.

Ingredients

1 LAMB'S TONGUE PER PERSON
1 LAMB'S BRAIN FOR 2 PEOPLE
1 ONION STUDDED WITH CLOVES
1 CARROT
1 SPRIG THYME
1 BAY LEAF
OLIVE OIL, BALSAMIC VINEGAR
BUTTER, FLOUR
SALT, PEPPER
FINES HERBES
YOUNG LETTUCES

- Cook tongues in water with onion, carrot, thyme, bay, salt and pepper. Simmer for between 1 hour and 1 1/2 hours.
- Meanwhile, soak brain(s) in cold water until white.

Poach in salted water with a few drops of vinegar (bring to boil then leave to cool in the cooking liquor).

- Peel tongues. This should be easy. If it is not, the tongues are not sufficiently cooked. Trim off rear part of tongues and slice remainder in two lengthways.
- Drain and quarter brain(s).

Place some butter and olive oil in a frying pan. Dust brains with flour and fry until golden on all sides (the flour adds a bit of "bite"). Remove onto a baking tray.

- Fry tongue(s) without dusting in flour first.
- Lay out young lettuces in the middle of a large serving dish and surround by alternating tongues and brains. Season with vinaigrette and a few fines herbes.

This is a good springtime hors d'œuvre accompanied by a Rosé de Tavel or a Rosé de Lirac. A real delight!

Fish

BOUILLABAISSE

Ingredients

3 KG RED SOUP
1 LEEK
1 HEAD FENNEL
3 WHOLE GARLIC (HALVED)
1 ONION
250 G TOMATO PUREE
2 G SAFFRON
THYME, BAY

Fish Soup

•Sweat all vegetables without allowing to colour. Add fish (red soup), tomato puree and saffron. Stir well until fish falls to pieces. Cover with water and cook for 3 hours at a slow rolling boil. Strain through a Chinese sieve (not too fine mesh). Correct seasoning (salt, pepper) than keep hot. There should be at least 5 litres stock left.

Ingredients

5 MEDIUM-SIZED MULLET (200 G PER FISH)
2 JOHN DORY FILLETS (500 G PER FILLET), CUT INTO 10 PORTIONS
5 WEEVERS (100 G PER WEEVER)
1 SMALL CONGER EEL (CUT INTO SLICES OF APPROX. 80 G EACH)
5 MEDIUM-SIZED SCORPION FISH (200 G EACH)
5 RED GURNARD (200 G EACH)

Fish

•Take three wide-necked sauté pans. In one, place red gurnard and weevers; in another, scorpion fish and mullet; in the third conger eel and John Dory.

Pour over olive oil and sprinkle with fine sea salt. Then pour in enough soup to barely cover fish and begin to cook. Once fish is cooked, keep hot.

ROAST COD

Serves 4

1 PIECE COD (600 G)
4 TOMATOES
GARLIC
PARSLEY
SEA SALT
OLIVE OIL, BALSAMIC VINEGAR
SALT, PEPPER
FLOUR

•Rub piece of cod with sea salt and leave for 1 hour in a clean teatowel.

•Meanwhile, slice tomatoes fairly thickly. Dust with flour and fry in olive oil until golden. Remove immediately from pan and drain on kitchen paper.

•Finely chop garlic and parsley. Preheat oven (180°C).

•Carefully wash cod under cold water to remove salt. Drain and dry then cut into four fillets. Lay fillets in a dish and pour on olive oil.

•Roast fish in the oven, with skin uppermost, for 8 to 10 minutes. Arrange sliced tomato on a serving dish.

•As soon as fish is cooked, switch off oven and put tomatoes in oven to keep warm. Remove skin from cod and lay fish out over sliced tomatoes.

•Recover cooking liquor from fish, add a few drops balsamic vinegar, chopped parsley and garlic. Pour sauce over fish to serve.

Bouillabaisse

RED MULLET WITH FENNEL

Serves 6

Rock mullet, as our local fishermen often say, is the "snipe of the sea". And, like snipe, it requires very little to make it very tasty as long as it is freshly caught.

6 PIECES MULLET (250 TO 300 G EACH)
3 FENNEL
1 ONION
1 CARROT
2 CLOVES GARLIC
1 G SAFFRON
25 CL WHITE WINE
THYME, BAY LEAF, SALT, PEPPER, OLIVE OIL

•Braise fennel with saffron (see recipe in the chapter on Vegetables).

•Fillet mullet and grill with skin side down in a very hot frying pan. Turn and cook for only a few minutes on the fleshy side.

•Serve piping hot with fennel as a garnish, moistened with vinaigrette and washed down with a good bottle of white Côtes-du-Rhône.

Serves 6

6 RED MULLET
6 ITALIAN TOMATOES (RIPE BUT FIRM)
3 SHALLOTS
12 BLACK OLIVES
BALSAMIC VINEGAR, OLIVE OIL
A FEW SPRIGS DILL

RED MULLET WITH FRIED ITALIAN TOMATOES

•Prepare mullet fillets, removing bones with tweezers.

•Skin tomatoes. Cut lengthways, remove seeds and season with salt. Drain.

•Meanwhile, finely chop shallots. Stone olives and chop roughly with a knife.

•Prepare a vinaigrette with olive oil, balsamic vinegar, salt and pepper.

•Fry tomatoes with olive oil. Add shallots. Leave to relax then lay out on plates.

•Fry red mullets skin side down then turn over and fry on fleshy side. Do not overcook. Lay on tomatoes.

•Decorate with sprigs of dill and chopped black olives. Pour on vinaigrette.

Red Mullet with Fried Italian Tomatoes

Mushroom-Stuffed Calamaries

MUSHROOM-STUFFED CALAMARIES

"Supions" are small calamaries which are superb as a starter or main course. They take some time to prepare.

This is the recipe for calamaries stuffed with penny bun mushrooms, a very tasty dish.

Serves 4 to 6

200 TO 300 G CALAMARIES
500 G PENNY BUN MUSHROOMS
20 G POWDERED PENNY BUN MUSHROOMS
500 G CULTIVATED MUSHROOMS
3 SHALLOTS (FINELY CHOPPED)
2 CLOVES GARLIC
10 G FRESH PARSLEY (CHOPPED)
OLIVE OIL

- Dice penny bun mushrooms and fry in oil seasoned with salt and pepper. Drain in a colander or sieve.
- Finely chop cultivated mushrooms. Sauté shallots with a small quantity of olive oil. When shallots are golden, add cultivated mushrooms and cook until liquor has reduced away. Leave to cool then mix penny buns, cultivated mushrooms, dried penny bun mushrooms, finely chopped garlic and parsley.
- Check seasoning. The stuffing is ready.
- Clean calamaries. Pull head away to gut and remove legs and rinse well in cold water. Drain and dry slightly on an electric ring.
- Cut legs at eye level (eyes are discarded) and chop roughly. Fry and blend into stuffing.
- Fill calamaries using an icing bag and close with a toothpick. Fry in a hot frying pan until golden on each side. Complete cooking by baking for a few minutes in the oven.

Calamaries can be served as they are with a side salad and good herb vinaigrette or with a crab coulis and a little grated parmesan cheese.

SOLE AND VEGETABLE TURNOVERS

Serves 4

4 FILLETS OF SOLE
1 CARROT
1 SHALLOT
1 STICK CELERY
1 ONION
PUFF PASTRY

- Finely dice vegetables and fry gently in butter. Season with salt and pepper.
- Preheat the oven.
- Roll out puff pastry.
- Flatten and dry fillets of sole. Top with diced vegetables. Roll up and enclose in puff pastry to form a turnover. Seal edges, prick top with a fork and brush with egg yolk.
- Put turnovers on a lightly-floured baking tray and bake for 15 minutes at 180°C.

Lobster

LOBSTER WITH ORANGE BUTTER AND CHINESE ANISE

•Bring salted water containing vinegar to the boil in a large saucepan. When boiling, place lobsters in pan. N.B. The lobsters must be alive. Cover pan to avoid splashes. Cook for no more than 2 minutes after water has returned to the boil. Remove lobster from water and leave to cool on a baking tray.

•Meanwhile, squeeze oranges and strain juice through a fine-meshed sieve. Reduce down until juice resembles a fairly liquid syrup then blend in butter as if making a white butter sauce. Add Chinese anise and set aside.

•Cut strips of courgettes and carrots. Cook for a few minutes in salted water but be careful - they cook very quickly. Cool in iced water to ensure that courgettes remain green.

•Remove lobster from shell, including tail and pincers. Keep carcasses to make something else (e.g. lobster coulis or American Sauce). Cut tail in two lengthways.

•Fry everything in olive oil. Lobster should be slightly browned to improve its taste.

•Lay lobster on plates, arrange vegetables on top or round about and pour on orange butter.

Serves 2

2 LOBSTER (600 TO 650 G)
4 ORANGES
2 G GROUND CHINESE ANISE
300 G BUTTER
2 COURGETTES
1 CARROT
8 SMALL SPRING ONIONS

GRILLED LOBSTER WITH TARRAGON BUTTER

•It is true that lobster is excellent when simply grilled. Cut in half, remove central gut and gravel sack in top of head. Break pincers with a heavy knife and grill, beginning with the fleshy side so that it cooks first and remains in place in shell. Cook for a few minutes then turn over onto shell and finish cooking over a low heat. Cooking time varies according to size but should never exceed 10 to 15 minutes.

•Cook shallots with white wine and an equal quantity of water. When the liquid has reduced by two-thirds, gradually whisk in butter. When sauce is smooth (like a white butter sauce), add tarragon.

Enjoy this dish with a good bottle of Châteauneuf-du-Pape from La Gardine-Vieilles-Vignes.

Tarragon Butter

1 FINELY CHOPPED SHALLOT
10 G CHOPPED TARRAGON
1/2 GLASS WHITE WINE
200 G BUTTER

Lobster with Orange Butter and Chinese Anise

Tuna Fish

Tuna fish, as we are often reminded, is the "steak of the sea" and it is true that it resembles meat to look at. These recipes only refer to red tuna fish.

Ask your fishmonger to give you some good steaks 3 to 4 cm (1 or 2 inches) thick weighing 130 to 150 g each depending on your appetite.

GRILLED TUNA FISH WITH MIXED PEPPERS

Serves 6

6 TUNA STEAKS
1 RED PEPPER
1 YELLOW PEPPER
1 GREEN PEPPER
1 LARGE ONION (FINELY CHOPPED)
1 CLOVE GARLIC
BALSAMIC VINEGAR AND OLIVE OIL

• Finely dice peppers and blanch in salted water. Cool immediately in iced water.

• Sweat onions in olive oil, add peppers and crushed garlic. Brown slightly.

• Grill tuna steaks, being careful not to overcook as tuna can rapidly become dry. Lay steaks on peppers.

Pour on vinaigrette.

Enjoy this dish with a good Tavel produced by the Roudil family.

TUNA FISH SLICE WITH AUBERGINES AND TOMATOES

Serves 6

3 LONG AUBERGINES
4 ITALIAN TOMATOES
1 ONION (FINELY CHOPPED)
2 CLOVES GARLIC (CRUSHED)
THYME, BAY LEAF, OLIVE OIL, SALT, PEPPER
50 CL CRUSHED, PUREED TOMATOES
10 G TARRAGON

• Slice aubergines into rounds and fry.

• Slice tomatoes fairly thickly and fry. When coloured on one side, add garlic, onion and thyme. Season with salt and pepper.

• Turn over and cook for a few seconds. Set aside on a drainage dish or kitchen paper.

• Cut tuna fish into slices thicker than fried aubergines and arrange in alternating layers in a round baking tin, beginning with tomatoes and ending with aubergines.

• Place in an oven preheated to 180°C and heat through.

• The slice is at its tastiest if it reaches a temperature of 60°C at the centre. Remove from the baking tin and serve with piping hot pureed tomatoes flavoured with tarragon.

Grilled Tuna Fish with Mixed Peppers

Scorpion Fish with Potato Gratin

Scorpion fish

Scorpion fish is very tasty. I advise you to buy it filleted because it has a very large head and there is, therefore, a lot of waste.

However, you can always use the head and bones to make a fish stock and use the stock in a vegetable gratin.

SCORPION FISH WITH POTATO GRATIN

Serves 6

- Sweat onion in a large gratin dish or baking tray until transparent.
- Meanwhile, finely slice potatoes (slightly thicker than crisps) and dust filets of scorpion fish with flour. Fry rapidly until lightly golden over a very high heat, taking care not to cook through. Lay out on the gratin dish.
- In a bowl, mix tomato, potatoes, thyme, bay and crushed cloves garlic. Cover scorpion fish with mixture. Arrange potatoes neatly on top then pour on sufficient fish stock to cover.
- Bake in a hot oven (180°C) for 30 to 40 minutes. To check whether everything is cooked, press on a potato.
- Serve piping hot with a dry white Côtes-du-Rhône.

6 FILLETS OF SCORPION FISH (100 TO 120 G EACH)
6 LARGE, FIRM POTATOES (120 TO 150 G PER PERSON)
100 G BLACK OLIVES (STONED)
200 G DICED RAW TOMATO
1 ONION (FINELY CHOPPED)
5 CLOVES GARLIC
SALT, PEPPER, OLIVE OIL

POACHED SCORPION FISH

Serves 4

- Boil vegetables and herbs. Strain off stock and cool vegetables.
- Place scorpion fish in a fish kettle, belly downmost. Pour on warm stock and gently bring to boil for 2 to 3 minutes depending on size of fish.
- Place lid on kettle and leave until almost cold (up to 50 minutes). The fish should be cooked and have a mouthwatering aroma.
- Serve with a few boiled vegetables, a good aïoli and a bottle of well chilled Rosé de Provence.

1 SCORPION FISH (2 TO 2.5 KG)
1 COURT-BOUILLON MADE WITH:
2 LITRES WATER
1 CARROT (SLICED)
1 ONION (SLICED)
2 SPRIGS CELERY (GREEN)
1 WHOLE GARLIC
3 CHINESE STARS
SALT, PEPPER
THYME, BAY LEAF

Sea Dace

Sea Dace is without doubt one of the most highly-prized fish in the south of France. It can reach a weight of 7 or 8 kg or more, although I have not seen a larger one for a long time. In my opinion, the best weight is 3 kg if you want to serve several people. However, smaller dace are also very tasty and, for two people, 800 g to 1 kg is sufficient.

DACE STEAKS WITH RATATOUILLE AND BLACK OLIVES

Serves 6

1 LARGE SEA DACE (3 TO 4 KG)
OLIVE OIL
RATATOUILLE
(SEE RECIPE UNDER "VEGETABLES")
A FEW BLACK OLIVES

- Fillet the sea dace or, as it is a fairly difficult job, ask the fishmonger to do it for you.
- Cut three good-sized steaks in each fillet. Place on an oiled baking sheet and bake in a hot oven (180°c) for 10 to 15 minutes, skin side uppermost.
- Leave the fish to relax for 10 minutes in its own stock.
- Heat the ratatouille after adding black olives. Serve piping hot.

BAKED DACE WITH PRESERVED TOMATOES

Serves 6 to 8

1 SEA DACE (3 KG)
2 KG PRESERVED TOMATOES
50 CL WHITE WINE
1 LITRE FISH STOCK
SALT, PEPPER, OLIVE OIL

- Lay dace on its side on a baking tray. Season with salt and pepper then slash along backbone so that it cooks quickly and does not break in the middle. Dribble on a small quantity of olive oil.
- Pour white wine into baking tray and place in an oven preheated to 180°C. Baste occasionally with fish stock. The baking tray should not be too dry but avoid pouring in too much stock as this would cause the fish to boil.
- Bake for 35 to 40 minutes at given temperature then remove fish and lay on a serving dish.
- Reduce stock almost completely then add preserved tomatoes and some olive oil.

Serve with rice or steamed vegetables and a glass of white Château La Nerthe. Delicious!.

Dace Steaks with Ratatouille and Black Olives

Small Dace

Serves 2

1 SEA DACE (800 G TO 1 KG)
200 G BUTTER
1 CHINESE ANISE
20 G WILD FENNEL
1 LEMON (JUICE ONLY)
SALT, PEPPER

I advise you to grill them for 15 to 20 minutes on a grill or in the oven with nothing but a little olive oil. Garnish with fennel-flavoured butter. A mouthwatering dish.

- Finely dice fennel and crush Chinese anise. Place in a saucepan with lemon juice and half-a-glass of water.
- Reduce down as if making a white butter sauce then gradually beat in butter.
- Pour over grilled dace for a wonderful taste.
- Garnish with braised fennel.

John Dory

This is a very fine fish. Small ones, weighing between 600 g and 1 kg, can be baked whole in the oven with a few herbs. Larger fish should be filleted. There is a lot of waste with this fish so allow 300 g to 400 g per person.

John Dory Wellington

Serves 6

6 FILLETS OF JOHN DORY (REMOVE SKIN FIRST)
2 POTATOES (USE A GOOD MASHING VARIETY)
1 SHALLOT (FINELY CHOPPED)
1 GLASS WHITE WINE
300 G BUTTER
20 G DICED PRESERVED LEMON
1 PIECE GINGER

- Slice potatoes very thinly as if making crisps.
- Do not wash potatoes; it is the starch in them which ensures that they cling to the fish.
- Grate ginger over John Dory and rub in (do not use too much; there should be just enough ginger to add flavour).
- Lay potatoes over fillets like fish scales.
- Heat oil and a small knob of butter in a frying pan.
- Begin frying fillets with potato side downwards.
- Once potatoes are golden brown, carefully turn fillets over and complete cooking, over a low heat.
- Meanwhile, reduce white wine with shallots and beat in butter as if making a white butter sauce.

Correct seasoning. Add diced preserved lemon just before serving.

- Serve fillets with potato side uppermost and pour butter round about.

John Dory Wellington

John Dory with Artichokes

John Dory with Artichokes

- Sweat shallots in a sauté pan then add artichokes, crushed garlic, thyme, bay leaf, carrots and a little water.

Cover with a lid and cook over a low heat.

- When three-quarters cooked, season fillets with salt and pepper and lay over artichokes.

- Cook, with lid on, for a further 5 to 8 minutes depending on thickness of fillets.

By cooking the fish in this way, it soaks up the taste of the artichokes.

Lay fillets on a serving dish or on individual plates and surround with artichokes.

- Make a vinaigrette with remaining stock.

This dish is quick to make and very tasty when served with a good white Côtes-du-Rhône.

Serves 6

6 FILLETS OF JOHN DORY (150 G TO 180 G) WITH SKIN LEFT ON
12 PURPLE ARTICHOKES (QUARTERED)
4 SHALLOTS (QUARTERED LENGTHWAYS)
1 CARROT (THINLY-SLICED)
THYME, BAY
3 CLOVES GARLIC (CRUSHED)
OLIVE OIL, SALT, PEPPER

Sole with Asparagus

Sole is a fish with an excellent flavour. Nobody ever tires of sole and there are a thousand and one ways of preparing it. Cook it whole if small, or in fillets for larger fish.

Served "à la meunière" or poached, it is an easy fish to work with and is full of taste.

- Cook asparagus in well salted water and cool immediately in cold salted water.

- Cut asparagus tips slightly longer than the width of the fillets of sole.

- Wrap fillets of sole around asparagus tips.

- Stand in a sauté pan, on finely chopped shallots, with green asparagus tip uppermost.

- Pour in white wine and cook for 10 to 15 minutes over a low heat, with a lid on.

- Meanwhile, dice remainder of asparagus.

- Once sole is cooked, remove from pan and reduce cooking liquor by three-quarters.

- Whisk in butter.

- At the last moment, add diced asparagus, chopped herbs and lemon juice.

- Reheat all ingredients and lay sole on a serving dish with piping hot braised asparagus round about.

Serves 6

6 FILLETS OF SOLE (60 TO 80 G EACH)
36 GREEN ASPARAGUS (WELL PEELED)
2 SHALLOTS
25 CL DRY WHITE WINE
300 G BUTTER
20 G FINES HERBES (PARSLEY, TARRAGON, CHERVIL)
1 LEMON (JUICE ONLY)

Breaded Roast Fish with Garlic Mayonnaise

• Skin and trim monkfish, stick with a few cloves garlic and cover in breadcrumbs mixed with thyme.

• Bake in a low oven with olive oil and butter (180°C), basting often with cooking liquor.

• Crush garlic and a small pinch sea salt with a pestle and mortar.

When crushed garlic is smooth, add egg yolks and gradually blend in olive oil to produce required quantity.

• Remove monkfish from oven and place on a serving dish. The garlic mayonnaise should be served in a sauce boat.

Serves 2

1 MONKFISH (800 G TO 1 KG)
300 G BREADCRUMBS
20 G THYME
OLIVE OIL
6 CLOVES GARLIC
2 EGGS
100 G BUTTER
LEMON JUICE
SEA SALT

Royal Bream with Tomatoes and Fennel

• Prepare, gut, and rinse bream. Remove scales. Lay fish flat on a board. Slash deeply along back fin towards backbone. This facilitates cooking and ensures that fish cooks regularly. Rub salt into slash and stuff fish with preserved tomatoes.

• Preheat oven (160°C).

• Prepare and quarter fennel. Cook in lightly salted water, turning off heat before fennel is completely cooked (the fennel is "blanched" to ensure that it then cooks correctly with tomatoes).

• Slice tomatoes and lay in an ovenproof dish. Finally chop fennel and scatter over tomatoes then top with stuffed bream. Pour on white wine, olive oil, grated nutmeg and coriander seeds. Season with salt and pepper and cook for 20 minutes.

• Remove and set aside fish. Reduce garnish to a rough puree of fennel and tomatoes.

Set portions of fish on hot individual plates with a portion of stuffing. Top with vegetable puree.

Dribble on olive oil just before serving.

Serves 6

1 ROYAL BREAM (1 TO 1.2 KG)
150 G PRESERVED TOMATOES
1 KG UNCOOKED TOMATOES (MARMANDE TYPE)
25 CL GOOD WHITE WINE
2 FENNEL
SALT, PEPPER
NUTMEG, CORIANDER SEEDS
OLIVE OIL

Breaded Roast Fish with Garlic Mayonnaise

Meat dishes

ROAST PARTRIDGE WITH CABBAGE CHARTREUSE

Serves 4

2 PARTRIDGE
1 SAVOY CABBAGE
2 ONIONS (CHOPPED)
2 CARROTS (CHOPPED)
100 G DICED GAMMON
5 CLOVES GARLIC

• Quarter cabbage. Remove stalks from middle and set aside green leaves. Braise white leaves with chopped onions and carrots, and gammon which has previously sweated. Bake for 2 hours in an oven at 130 to 150 °C.

• Roast partridge with cloves of garlic for 5 minutes on each wing and 5 minutes on the back. Leave partridge to rest for at least 10 minutes. Bone and set aside breast fillets in the fatty liquor produced by the bird during cooking. If legs are still pink, grill slightly.

• Break up carcass and make some good-flavoured stock by just covering with water and cooking until liquor has reduced by half. Strain liquor through a Chinese sieve and set aside.

• Meanwhile, use a 5 cm (2 inch) mould 3 to 4 cm (1 1/4 to 1 3/4 inches) in height to make a cabbage chartreuse. Line with green cabbage leaves. Braise and recook in a hot oven (150 to 160 °C) for 30 minutes.

• Lay the partridge breasts in a serving dish or on individual plates with legs on the side and piping hot gravy round about.

• Serve with a good Châteauneuf-du-Pape or a red Gigondas.

DUCK WITH PENNY BUN MUSHROOMS

Serves 6

6 DUCK THIGHS
1.5 KG PENNY BUN MUSHROOMS
1 SHALLOT (FINELY CHOPPED)
PARSLEY, 2 CLOVES GARLIC
50 CL CHICKEN STOCK
150 G BUTTER

• Fry duck thighs.

• Brown well on all sides. Remove any fat and add shallot and garlic.

• Once shallot is well browned, pour in chicken stock and cook until completely reduced.

• Sauté mushrooms in a frying pan and drain. Set aside mushroom liquor. Return mushrooms to pan and fry again. Season with salt and pepper. Mushrooms should be well coloured.

• Add mushroom liquor to duck.

• Reduce by half again and blend in butter.

• Add mushrooms and chopped parsley just before serving.

• Heat well and enjoy the meal with a good glass of Gigondas.

Roast Partidge with Cabbage Chartreuse

Avignon-Style Stew

AVIGNON-STYLE STEW

- Cut a boned leg of lamb into pieces approximately 90 g each in weight.
- Place a piece of diced bacon in each piece, taking care to insert along the direction of the fibres in the meat. The bacon should be seasoned with spiced salt.

- Marinate pieces of meat for 2 hours with 10 cl oil per litre of wine, chopped carrots and onions, four cloves garlic, thyme, bay, and parsley stalks.

- Chop three onions and mix with two crushed cloves garlic. Blanch 250 g finely-diced gammon.

- Cut 250 g fresh bacon rind into 2 cm (almost 1 inch) squares. Blanch.

- Place dried orange peel in a bunch of parsley.

- Line base and sides of a terrine with thin strips of pork fat. Add pieces of lamb, alternating layers of meat with layers of onion, bacon and rind. Sprinkle thyme and powdered bay leaf over each layer.

- Place bunch of parsley in the middle of the terrine and season each layer lightly.

- Strain marinade through a Chinese sieve and pour over meat and vegetables. Seal the terrine and ensure that the steam is concentrated.

- Begin cooking on the hob then bake for 5 hours in a low oven, ensuring that the oven temperature does not vary during the cooking time.

- When ready to serve, take off lid, remove pork fat, remove any excess fat and take out the bunch of parsley.

- The stew is served as is, in the terrine.

This is a rather long dish to prepare. The older generation used to bake it in the hearth. However, with a little time and a lot of love for dishes served with sauces, the recipe is a sure winner.

Duck Breast with Cherries

- Fry bones until well browned. Add vegetables (onions, carrot, garlic, celery).

- Cover with water and simmer gently for 2 hours skimming occasionally to remove any impurities that rise to the surface.

- Strain through a Chinese sieve and reduce to obtain half a litre of fairly thick, golden gravy.

- Meanwhile, remove some of the fat from duck breasts and sauté, beginning with fatty side down. The meat should be rare.

- Leave to rest.

- Degrease and deglaze with vinegar. Add cherries and duck stock.

- Bring to boil.

- Serve duck sliced and covered with piping hot gravy. A good glass of Saint-Estève des Côtes-du-Rhône is an excellent accompaniment.

Serves 4

4 DUCK BREASTS (300 TO 400 G)
200 G FROZEN OR CANNED CHERRIES
50 CL DUCK STOCK
1 GLASS BALSAMIC VINEGAR

Duck stock

3 KG DUCK CARCASS (CHOP CARCASS UP WELL)
2 ONIONS (ROUGHLY DICED)
1 CARROT (ROUGHLY DICED)
1 STICK CELERY (FINELY CHOPPED)
2 CLOVES GARLIC (CRUSHED)

Ox cheek

Serves 6

1.2 KG OX CHEEK
100 G CARROTS
100 G ONIONS
200 G SHALLOTS
150 G SPRING ONIONS
150 G CULTIVATED MUSHROOMS
BOUQUET GARNI
150 G GARLIC
1 LITRE CHÂTEAUNEUF-DU-PAPE
FLOUR

- Remove nerves and fat from ox cheeks then seal by frying quickly. Set aside.
- Fry carrots cut into sticks, chopped onions, shallots and halved whole garlic. Add ox cheeks then dust with flour.
- Pour in Châteauneuf-du-Pape and add water if necessary to cover ingredients. Add bouquet garni then cook for 4 hours at 150 °C.
- Remove pieces of meat, strain stock and reduce down to thicken.
- Add spring onions (browned) and fried mushrooms.
- Pour piping hot over meat.

This dish can be eaten with mashed potatoes or pasta because the "gravy" is very highly seasoned. It is excellent with a Châteauneuf-du-Pape.

Saddle of Hare with Jugged Gravy

Ingredients

1 SADDLE OF HARE FOR 2 PEOPLE
25 CL JUGGED GRAVY
4 CLOVES GARLIC
THYME, OIL, BALSAMIC VINEGAR
6 BOILED POTATOES TO GARNISH
BAY LEAF

Jugged gravy

1 KG GAME TRIMMINGS (ASK YOUR BUTCHER FOR THESE)
2 LARGE ONIONS
1 STICK CELERY
3 CLOVES GARLIC
1 CARROT
THYME, BAY
2 LITRES CÔTES-DU-RHÔNE (MADE FROM SYRAH GRAPES) OR ANY OTHER FULL-BODIED WINE
2 CLOVES, 5 JUNIPER BERRIES, 80 G FLOUR

- Fry game trimmings until brown.
- Fry onions and carrots until golden.
- Blend thyme, bay, celery and garlic with trimmings.
- Add cloves and juniper berries and sprinkle on flour.
- Cook for a few minutes. Pour on wine.
- Simmer for 4 hours over a low heat.
- Strain gravy and reduce by half to produce a black, smooth gravy.
- Remove nerves from saddle of hare. Roast in a sauté pan. Brown on all sides. Add garlic, thyme and bay.
- Finish cooking in a very hot oven (180 - 200°C). This takes between 10 and 15 minutes. The meat should be pink.
- Remove from oven and leave to rest.
- Degrease sauté pan, add half a glass of balsamic vinegar. Reduce and add one quarter litre of jugged gravy. Cook over a very low heat for 5 to 6 minutes. Strain through fine-meshed Chinese sieve, taking care to crush cloves of garlic.
- Correct seasoning. Reheat hare then remove bones. Serve in pieces, covered with gravy, and accompanied by boiled potatoes. This dish is excellent with a good Gigondas.

Ox cheek

Lamb and Aubergines

LAMB AND AUBERGINES

- Sauté neck of lamb. Use bones to make stock.
- At the same time, fry pieces of meat and add onions garlic, thyme and bay beef.
- Dice courgettes and tomatoes. Cook over a low heat for 2 hours with white wine.
- Thinly slice aubergine (lengthways), fry in olive oil then line small round moulds (for individual servings) or a gratin dish for a family meal.
- Place stew in the middle, cover with remainder of sliced aubergine.
- Complete cooking over a low heat for 30 minutes until tender.
- Serve with lamb gravy. Bind with few cloves garlic.

Serves 8

1.2 KG NECK OF LAMB (BONED BUT KEEP BONES TO MAKE STOCK)
8 LARGE RIPE TOMATOES
8 LARGE RIPE AUBERGINES
2 COURGETTES
1 WHOLE GARLIC
2 LARGE ONIONS
1 GLASS DRY WHITE WINE
THYME, BAY
OLIVE OIL, SALT, PEPPER (GROUND)

GUINEA FOWL SUPREME STUFFED WITH FOIE GRAS

- Flatten slices of breast. Remove the small nerve running through the fillets.
- Cut wings to remove all bones (set aside for sauce).
- Flatten fillets to make escalopes that are not too thin. Season with salt and pepper.
- Cut foie gras into four equal pieces (50 g each). Roll them slightly to form a sausage shape. Wrap escalope round foie gras and roll tightly in clingfilm.
- Poach, in clingfilm, for 30 to 40 minutes depending on size, in stock. N.B. Do not allow to boil.
- Meanwhile, make gravy with wings. Fry until golden with all trimmings in a large saucepan. When wings are golden brown, add onions, garlic and diced carrots and cook until golden. Be careful not to burn the juices that run from meat and vegetables.
- Degrease and deglaze with glass of port. Reduce then pour in enough stock to cover bones. Cook for 30 minutes, skimming to remove any impurities that float up to the surface. Strain the gravy and reduce again by half over a low heat.
- The fillets will now be cooked. Remove clingfilm and place fillets on a large serving dish.
- At the last minute, check the gravy, correct seasoning and gently blend in 100 g butter. Pour over fillets.

This dish can be eaten with boiled rice or spelt.

Serves 4

4 SLICES BREAST OF GUINEA FOWL FROM DRÔME
200 G FOIE GRAS
SALT, PEPPER
1 GLASS PORT
1 LITRE CHICKEN STOCK
1 ONION
3 CLOVES GARLIC
1 CARROT
100 G BUTTER

SHOULDER OF PORK WITH LENTILS

This is an ideal recipe for a festive meal with family or friends. You can make it well in advance. It is a hearty meal, one that encourages guests to sit back and enjoy the convivial company.

Serves 6 to 8

1 HALF-SALTED SHOULDER OF PORK
500 G GREEN LENTILS
1 CARROT
1 ONION STUCK WITH 3 CLOVES
3 CLOVES GARLIC
1 BOUQUET GARNI (THYME, BAY, STICK OF CELERY)
OLIVE OIL AND A FEW DROPS VINEGAR

• Remove some of the salt from shoulder of pork by soaking in cold water for 2 or 3 hours. Place in a large saucepan with garlic, carrots, bouquet garni and onion. Pour in enough cold water to cover and simmer for 2 hours over a low heat.

• Place lentils in another saucepan and cook in cooking liquor from pork. Do not overcook. 15 to 20 minutes are sufficient; the lentils should remain slightly crisp. Once cooked, drain. The cooking liquor can be served as a lentil consommé, a very tasty soup.

• Add a few drops vinegar and a good quantity of olive oil.

• Bone shoulder of pork (this should be easy to do) and serve piping hot with mustard. Superb!

FRICASSEE OF POULTRY WITH SHERRY VINEGAR

Fricassee of poultry is a fairly quick dish to prepare. If you use Sherry Vinegar, the gravy will be slightly more acid than with balsamic vinegar so, if you prefer a milder taste, replace the sherry vinegar by an equal quantity of balsamic vinegar.

Serves 4 to 6

1 CHICKEN (1.8 TO 2 KG)
5 LEEKS
1 LITRE DOUBLE CREAM
25 CL SHERRY VINEGAR
2 SHALLOTS
50 G BUTTER

• Cut chicken into eight pieces. Lightly brown in a large sauté pan in hot butter, taking care not to let the meat burn. When the chickn has turned golden, remove remaining butter which may be slightly black. Add finely chopped shallots and sweat for a few minutes.

• Put pieces of chicken back in pan and add vinegar. Reduce by one-half then add cream and simmer gently for 10 minutes. Remove white meat and continue cooking legs for a further 10 minutes.

• Meanwhile, cut leeks into sections 10 cm (4 inches) in length and cook in salted water. Cool in iced water as soon as they are cooked.

• Lay on a serving dish and top with pieces of poultry.

• Reduce sauce slightly and blend in a liquidiser till smooth.

• Pour hot over the chicken.

Serve this dish with a good wine.

Shoulder of Pork with Lentils

JUGGED HARE

The best hares for cooking purposes are hares born during the year. They weigh between 2.5 and 3 kg. However, for Jugged Hare, an animal more than a year old weighing 4 to 5 kg is equally suitable and it is sometimes cheaper.

Jugged Hare

•Cut hare into fairly large pieces. Remove gall and set aside liver. Keep any blood remaining inside the animal.

•Marinate pieces of meat with onions, carrots, and cubed celery. Add wine to cover and season with herbs and spices. Leave to marinate for one day in a cool place.

•The next day, drain pieces of meat and keep marinade.

•In a large saucepan, fry vegetables in olive oil. Brown pieces of hare in a frying pan. Lay out in the saucepan with vegetables. Add flour, stir well, pour on wine from marinade, season with salt and pepper and cook for 2 hours in a low oven.

•Meanwhile, finely chop liver and mix with remaining blood.

•When meat is cooked, remove from sauce and correct seasoning. If the sauce is slightly acid, continue cooking for a few minutes.

•Prepare a garnish with 150 g spring onions lightly cooked until almost golden, 150 g gammon (diced, blanched and sautéed until crisp), 200 g cultivated mushrooms (quartered) of a size equivalent to the spring onions.

•Add this garnish (known as "grandmother's garnish") to the pieces of meat.

•At the last minute, add liver and blood to sauce to bind and give it a beautiful black colour. Pour over pieces of meat and gently heat.

•N.B. The sauce must not boil. If it does the blood will form lumps and the sauce will be much less tasty.

•Serve this superb dish with steamed potatoes or fresh pasta.

Serves 6 to 8

1 HARE
1 LITRE GOOD RED WINE (GIGONDAS OR CHÂTEAUNEUF-DU-PAPE)
2 CARROTS
2 ONIONS
6 CLOVES GARLIC
1 STICK CELERY
3 CLOVES
6 JUNIPER BERRIES
3 SPOONS FLOUR
THYME, BAY
OLIVE OIL

SADDLE OF RABBIT WITH LIVER STUFFING

•Bone saddle of rabbit, beginning by removing fillets. Remove bone without detaching flesh along back.

•Roughly dice liver, season with salt and pepper and dust with thyme.

•Place stuffing in centre of saddle. Roll in caul and tie up with string as if making a roast.

•Roast for 20 to 25 minutes in a very hot oven, with a whole garlic.

•Add 200 g preserved tomatoes at end of cooking time. Leave to rest.

•Deglaze with water or stock. Reduce down until clear and slightly "fatty".

Delicious served with a good red Gigondas.

Serves 2

1 SADDLE RABBIT
RABBIT'S LIVER
1 WHOLE GARLIC
200 G PRESERVED TOMATOES
SALT, PEPPER, THYME
CAUL
STOCK

LAMB STEW WITH SPRING VEGETABLES

Serves 6

1.5 KG SHOULDER OR NECK OF LAMB CUT INTO
LARGE PIECES, WITH BONES
2 LARGE ONIONS (FINELY CHOPPED)
1 KG RIPE TOMATOES (CUT INTO EIGHT)
4 CLOVES GARLIC
THYME, BAY
50 CL WHITE WINE

Garnish

200 G YOUNG CARROTS (WELL BLANCHED)
200 G YOUNG TURNIPS (WELL BLANCHED)
200 G SPRING ONIONS (LIGHTLY FRIED IN BUTTER)
100 G PEAS (COOKED IN WELL SALTED WATER)
150 G MANGE-TOUT PEAS (COOKED IN WELL SAL-
TED WATER BUT STILL CRISP)

For sautés and stews, I recommend shoulder or neck of lamb. They are excellent cuts for braising.

• To prepare stew, sauté pieces of lamb in a frying pan until brown. Place in stew pan large enough to contain all ingredients.

• Add onion (it should also be golden brown) then tomatoes and white wine, cloves of garlic (crushed), thyme and bay.

• Simmer for 1 1/2 to 2 hours depending on sizes of pieces of meat. If there is not enough cooking liquor, add water.

• Check seasoning.

• When meat is cooked, remove and place on a serving dish.

• Strain gravy through a Chinese sieve. Reheat all vegetables and lay out on top of the meat. Cover with piping hot gravy.

• Serve hot. This is a very pleasant springtime dish.

CROWN OF PORK WITH CHORISO

Serves 8

1 CROWN PORK (6 CHOPS)
200 G SLICES OF STRONG CHORISO (SPICY SAU-
SAGE)
1 ONION
1 CARROT
6 CLOVES GARLIC
THYME, BAY, SPRIG OF SAGE

• It is easier to ask your butcher to prepare the pork for you. Ask him to remove the bones at the bottom and make a break in the bones along the side of the crown.

• Roast in a roasting dish. Fry onions until golden, add carrots, garlic then place crown on top and add water until half-covered. Add thyme, bay and sage. Salt and pepper lightly and roast in a hot oven (200 to 210°C) for 45 minutes to 1 hour depending on the size of the roast, turning occasionally. The addition of plenty of water ensures that the meat is not dry and, if the oven is not as hot, it will brown anyway.

• Meanwhile, lay slices of choriso on two baking trays and grill in a hot oven. They should be crisp and have lost all their fat.

As an accompaniment to the crown of pork, here is a recipe for mashed potatoes and olives.

• Use potatoes of a variety recommended for mashing (150 g potatoes per person). Peel, cut into large cubes and cook, adding enough lightly salted water to cover potatoes but no more. When cooked, add single cream up to the halfway

Crown of Pork with Choriso

mark and continue cooking. The potatoes should be well cooked. They will almost be like a puree at this point. Finish mashing them with a fork and add 20 to 30 g of chopped black olives.

•When the crown of pork is cooked, cut into good slices, dot with slices of choriso to add a slightly spicy taste, and serve the mashed potato separately.

RABBIT WITH HERBS

• Preheat oven (200 to 210°C).

• Place rabbit in a baking dish large enough to contain rabbit and all herbs. Pour a good quantity of olive oil over rabbit and place in oven until browned on all sides.

Rabbit with Herbs

- After 5 to 10 minutes (ensure that rabbit is well browned), roll rabbit in aluminium foil to protect it and put all herbs in the bottom (do not add tomatoes as they are already cooked).

- Put back in oven at a lower temperature. Turn occasionally and stir herbs so that they release their full flavour.

- Cook for a further 5 to 10 minutes then remove rabbit from oven and leave to rest. Ensure that garlic and artichokes are well cooked then remove and degrease dish.

- Add a few drops of water to make a gravy. Add tomatoes, garlic and artichokes.

- Cut saddle in four, thighs in half. Serve piping hot.

Serves 6 to 8

1 HALF-RABBIT (SADDLE + 2 THIGHS)
10 CLOVES GARLIC (NOT PEELED)
200 G PRESERVED TOMATOES
THYME, BAY, SAGE
5 ARTICHOKE HEART (CUT INTO 8)
SALT, PEPPER, OLIVE OIL

GUINEA FOWL WITH OLIVES

Fricassee of guinea fowl with olives is fairly quick to prepare and it makes a delicious family meal if served with spelt or fresh pasta.

- Quarter guinea fowl. Cut legs in two to form drumsticks and thighs. Cut breasts in half. This gives eight equal pieces.

- Heat olive oil in a large sauté pan. Season pieces of meat and brown in oil. This initial browning is important for the flavour. The meat should be browned on all sides.

- Remove meat from pan and pour off fat. Add chopped shallot and fry until golden but not brown. Put pieces of meat back in pan and deglaze with white wine.

- Reduce gravy and add chicken stock. Cook for 10 to 15 minutes.

- Remove small pieces of breast which cook quickly. Leave remainder of meat in pan for a further 10 minutes at least.

- To check that the fowl is well cooked, prick with a fork or the tip of a knife blade. The liquid that runs out should be clear. If it is pink, the meat is not sufficiently cooked.

- Reduce chicken stock almost completely. There should be only enough liquid in the pan to cover the base. Add cream and cook until reduced by half. Add olives (quartered) and pieces of guinea fowl. Simmer for 5 minutes and serve piping hot.

Serves 8

1 GUINEA FOWL (1.8 TO 2 KG)
200 G GREEN OLIVES (STONED)
1 SHALLOT
1 LITRE STOCK
1 LITRE DOUBLE CREAM
25 CL WHITE WINE
OLIVE OIL, SALT, PEPPER

ROAST PIGEON WITH GARLIC

Serves 2

1 PIGEON (600 TO 650 G)
6 CLOVES GARLIC
SALT, PEPPER, THYME, BAY

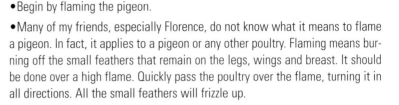

- Begin by flaming the pigeon.
- Many of my friends, especially Florence, do not know what it means to flame a pigeon. In fact, it applies to a pigeon or any other poultry. Flaming means burning off the small feathers that remain on the legs, wings and breast. It should be done over a high flame. Quickly pass the poultry over the flame, turning it in all directions. All the small feathers will frizzle up.
- Then gut the pigeon. Cut off neck and legs and set aside to make gravy. Place a bay leaf and sprig of thyme inside pigeon.
- Pot roast in a small pan scarcely bigger than the bird. Heat well then add neck and legs. Cook pigeon on one side (over a fairly strong heat) for 5 minutes then turn over and again cook for 5 minutes.
- Preheat oven to 180 to 200 °C. Put pigeon on its back, add cloves garlic and roast in the oven for 10 minutes.
- In Provence, pigeon is served slightly pink. If you prefer it well cooked, add 5 minutes to the roasting time.
- The pigeon should be golden brown when removed from oven. Leave to rest for 15 minutes to tenderise the meat.
- Degrease the saucepan and deglaze with a small glass water. Reduce down to a thick gravy.

Serve with thyme-flavoured potato cakes. This is a really mouthwatering dish.

CROWN OF LAMB IN SEA SALT

In Provence, lamb is the traditional choice for Easter Sunday.

The paschal lamb should not be too fat nor too pink. It should be almost white and very slightly veined.

Serves 2

1 CROWN LAMB (6 CHOPS) (ASK YOUR BUTCHER TO PREPARE THE CROWN ROAST AND GIVE YOU THE BONES)
1 ONION
1 CARROT
3 CLOVES GARLIC
THYME, BAY
SEA SALT

- Lay bones on a baking tray. Preheat oven and roast bones till brown.
- When bones are brown, rub crown roast with sea salt and lay over bones (skin side uppermost). Cook in the still hot oven for 10 minutes, basting to ensure that it colours evenly. Leave for a further 5 minutes.
- Remove and rest for 15 to 20 minutes on a dish, turning occasionally to ensure that the blood circulates through the entire roast.

Crown of Lamb in Sea Salt

•Meanwhile, remove any fat on baking tray and fry onions and carrots. Pour on water to make sauce, add thyme and bay and cook for a good half-hour. Strain through a fine Chinese sieve.

•Carve roast and moisten with gravy before serving. If crown roast has cooled, reheat before carving.

FEET AND TRIPE PARCELS

Ingredients

12 SMALL LAMB'S TRIPE PARCELS
6 LAMB'S FEET
1 PEPPER
1 KG TOMATOES
200 G CARROTS
300 G ONIONS
1 L WHITE WINE
OLIVE OIL

• Tripe parcels, known in the south of France as "paquets", are lamb's tripe stuffed with gammon, parsley and garlic, then cut into triangles, rolled up and tied with string. Personally, I recommend that you ask your tripe merchant to prepare them for you.

• Sweat vegetables with some olive oil. When golden brown, top with feet and tripe parcels.

• Add tomatoes last of all then season with salt and pepper and add pimento. Pour in 1 litre good white wine and bring up to the required level with water.

• Cook for 6 hours over a gentle heat. Once cooked, remove tripe parcels and feet.

• Recook sauce to remove any acidity.

This dish is served piping hot with boiled potatoes.

Feet and Tripe Parcels

**Grilled Lamb's Feet
with Truffle Stuffing**

GRILLED LAMB'S FEET WITH TRUFFLE STUFFING

•Blanch lamb's feet well. Cool in cold water then braise with carrots, onion, shallot, cloves, thyme, bay, salt and pepper. Add white wine and water until just covered. Braise in a low oven for 3 to 4 hours.

•Meanwhile, stew sweetbreads. Sweat chopped shallot and onion, add sweetbreads, and pour in 25 cl lamb stock. Cook for 1 hour then add truffles.

•Remove feet from pan, bone while still hot, lay out on a working surface and fill with truffle and sweetbread stew. Roll in caul to form "sausages". Leave overnight so that the ingredients soak up the various flavours.

•To serve, grill well then deglaze griddle pan with vinegar. Make a vinaigrette with lamb stock.

•Serve with boiled potatoes in the stock, washed down with a glass of white Coteaux d'Aix-en-Provence from Les Baux.

Serves 4

8 LAMB'S FEET
400 G LAMB'S SWEETBREADS (WELL BLANCHED AND WITH ALL NERVES REMOVED)
100 G TRUFFLES (TRIMMINGS)
1 ONION
1 SHALLOT
2 CARROTS
2 CLOVES
1 LITRE GOOD DRY WHITE WINE
50 CL LAMB STOCK
THYME, BAY, SALT, PEPPER
200 G CAUL (WELL WASHED)
OIL, VINEGAR

Vegetables

RATATOUILLE

Ratatouille is the all-time great Provençal dish and there is always some in the refrigerator during the summer. It can be eaten cold or hot and the vegetables can be cut in several different ways. Purists will tell you that they must be roughly diced; these days, chefs tend to dice the vegetables finely and avoid overcooking them. This method gives the vegetables more flavour and, more importantly, ensures that they retain their beautiful colours.

Serves 10

2 KG TOMATOES
600 G AUBERGINES
100 G COURGETTES
4 LARGE ONIONS
4 GREEN PEPPERS
6 CLOVES GARLIC
THYME, BAY, OLIVE OIL, SALT, PEPPER

•Finely dice all vegetables, beginning with peppers. Blanch for a few minutes in a good quantity of water (this makes them more digestible).

•Chop aubergines and courgettes, making sure that pieces are all the same size then sauté in a hot pan with olive oil. They should be allowed to colour slightly. Drain in a colander because the vegetables absorb a lot of oil (especially the aubergines). Keep oil to make vinaigrettes with. They will be full of flavour and aroma.

•Meanwhile, skin tomatoes, remove pips, then chop roughly with a large knife.

•Chop onions and sweat in a large pan until almost transparent. Add tomatoes and cook until liquor has almost reduced away. Add garlic, thyme, bay, salt and pepper.

•Mix in all the vegetables: courgettes, aubergines, tomatoes and peppers. Boil for a few minutes.

The ratatouille should retain a good colour and have a wonderful aroma. The vegetables should remain crisp. Ratatouille can be served with grilled fish and cold roast meats. It can also be eaten as a starter with a few slices of toast or with eggs.

Serve with red wine such as a Domaine de la Président, Sainte-Cécile-les-Vignes.

There is another way of preparing this marvellous dish, the so-called "Bohemian" method (a reference to Esmeralda for Victor Hugo fans and those who have enjoyed *Notre-Dame de Paris*).

Use the same quantities of ingredients as indicated above but add two fennel cut into pieces of the same size as the other vegetables. Blanch in the same way as the peppers then proceed as above. Bake the vegetables in a hot oven (150°C) until soft.

The fennel adds a touch of freshness and a hint of aniseed.

This is an excellent, fresh recipe which goes well with a Rosé de Tavel, Domaine du Vieux-Relais.

Ratatouille

White-Beet au Gratin

WHITE-BEET AU GRATIN

This vegetable (which is merely a large tuft of leaves on a large stem) is particularly delicious. It is available almost throughout the year and can be cooked in several different ways.

Serves 10

1 KG WHITE-BEET
180 G GRATED PARMESAN
1 LITRE BECHAMEL SAUCE (100 G BUTTER, 80 G FLOUR, 1 LITRE MILK, SALT, PEPPER, NUTMEG)

•Separate green leaves from stems. Wash green leaves well and cook for 10 minutes in salted water. Quickly cool in iced water. Drain and set aside.

•Peel stems, removing as many strings as possible. Cut into pieces 10 cm (4 inches) long and 0.5cm (1/4 inch) wide. Cook in salted water for 15 to 20 minutes. Cool, drain and set aside.

•Make bechamel sauce: melt butter then add flour and stir slowly with a wooden spoon. Bring milk to boil and gradually whisk into butter/flour roux. The sauce should be smooth and free from lumps. If lumps do form, strain through a Chinese sieve or liquidise. Cook for a few minutes.

•Meanwhile, finely chop green part of white-beet. Mix with stems and lay out in a gratin dish. Pour over bechamel sauce and sprinkle with grated parmesan. Bake in the oven until well browned (hot oven: 160 to 170°C).

This dish is an ideal accompaniment to roast meats, loin of veal or leg of lamb. I recommend a light red wine from Cairanne or Lirac.

White-beet can also be cooked in a frying pan. Use the same quantities and sauté in a frying pan with olive oil. Add a good quantity of chopped parsley and three cloves garlic.

It is an unusual, elegant vegetable to serve with left-overs or in chicken stock.

RED OR GREEN PEPPERS WITH OLIVE OIL

In summer, when peppers are in season, they are wonderful with olive oil. They can be served with an aperitif or as a garnish for patés and salads.

•Take red or green peppers, cut in half, remove seeds and place, open side uppermost, on a baking tray. Season with salt and pepper, sprinkle with oil, and place in a very hot oven (200 to 210°C) until the skins crack and become almost black.

•Remove from oven and cover with a teatowel. They are then very easy to peel.

•Place in a terrine and cover with oil, a small quantity of garlic and a few sprigs of thyme.

They can be served at any time, with toast made from a country loaf.

Turnips

Turnips no longer enjoy the place they once had in recipe books. In Provence, they are rarely part of our traditional dishes but I like them, especially young white turnips. This is why I am giving you the following recipe which brings out the full flavour of the vegetable. It is delicious served with red meats or grilled fish.

**Preserved Turnip
in Balsamic Vinegar**

Preserved Turnip in Balsamic Vinegar

- Peel turnips. N.B. in winter they have two skins, so peel thickly.
- Cut into rounds and blanch well in lightly salted water.
- In a large pan, reduce the vinegar by half. Add turnips and cook until vinegar has fully evaporated. The turnips will turn black.
- Add some pepper and olive oil - *et voilà!*
- This is an unusual but mouthwatering vegetable dish.

Serves 6

12 SMALL WHITE TURNIPS
25 CL BALSAMIC VINEGAR
SALT, PEPPER
2 SPOONS OLIVE OIL

Early Vegetables in Poulette Sauce

- Wash and peel vegetables. Shape artichoke hearts and cut into quarters. Cut celery and carrots into pieces of approximately the same size to improve the appearance of the dish. Cook separately in salted water and cool immediately by plunging into iced water.
- Make Poulette Sauce. Bring stock to boil and reduce by half. Blend in cream. Bring back to boil and pour over egg yolks, whisking as if making custard.
- Return to a gentle heat, being careful not to boil, and stir continuously. Gradually mix in butter. Add lemon juice and fines herbes.
- Reheat vegetables slightly and mix everything together.

Lay out on a serving dish. This is an excellent hors d'oeuvre with a white Châteauneuf-du-Pape wine.

Serves 6

1 KG PEAS
1 KG MANGE-TOUT PEAS
1 KG PURPLE ARTICHOKES
2 KG ASPARAGUS (OR 1 KG ASPARAGUS TIPS)
1 KG YOUNG CARROTS
1 HEAD CELERY
1 LITRE STOCK
3 EGG YOLKS
50 CL CREAM
100 G BUTTER
1 LEMON (JUICE ONLY)
FINES HERBES

Stewed Mange-Tout Peas with Bacon

- Fry bacon and chopped onions in olive oil. Add garlic and mange-tout peas with 50 cl beef stock and simmer over a low heat for 10 minutes. Season with salt and pepper. Lay out in a round and pour beef stock and preserved tomatoes on the outside.

Ingredients

1 KG MANGE-TOUT PEAS
100 G FRESH, DICED BACON
2 ONIONS
4 CLOVES GARLIC
50 CL BEEF STOCK
5 CL OLIVE OIL
50 G PRESERVED TOMATOES
SALT, PEPPER

Courgettes

This is a decidedly Mediterranean vegetable which can be long or round. People in Northern France only discovered it some fifty years ago. Because of this, they tend to peel it; in the South of France it is eaten with its skin.

MAGALI COURGETTES

Ingredients

6 BABY COURGETTES
3 LARGE RIPE TOMATOES
2 ONIONS
3 CLOVES GARLIC
THYME
1 BAY LEAF
SALT, PEPPER, OLIVE OIL

- Finely slice onions. Chop cloves garlic and lay in baking dish.
- Cut courgettes in fan shapes. Fill spaces with slices of tomato.
- Lay on a bed of onions. Season with salt and pepper, pour on olive oil and bake in a hot oven (180°C).

This vegetable goes very well with a crown of lamb or fried veal chops.

ROUND NICE COURGETTES STUFFED WITH MARJORAM

Ingredients

6 ROUND COURGETTES (80 TO 100 G)
1 ONION (CHOPPED)
2 CLOVES GARLIC (CHOPPED)
30 G MARJORAM
2 EGG YOLKS
2 SPOONS DOUBLE CREAM
OLIVE OIL

- Cut courgettes one-third down from the stalk end. Spoon out interior (taking care not to perforate the skin). Blanch in salted water, with their "hats".

Meanwhile, sweat onion in a small quantity of olive oil. When onion is transparent, add courgette flesh and simmer until liquor has reduced away. Stir frequently to form a sort of puree. Add cream.

- Reduce further, almost by half. Cool. Mix in egg yolks, and check seasoning. Add chopped marjoram.
- Dry courgettes well with a teatowel or kitchen paper. Fill with stuffing and replace "hats". Bake in an oven at 160°C. Pour on some olive oil and cook for 2 to 2 1/2 hours. The stuffing is cooked when it resembles an egg custard.

The courgettes can be eaten hot with a herb vinaigrette or cold. They are as delicious with large cuts of meat as with a rib of beef.

Magali Courgettes

Courgettes and Preserved Tomatoes

Courgettes and Preserved Tomatoes

- Skin tomatoes, quarter and remove pips. Drain.
- Meanwhile, slice courgettes approximately 1 cm (1/2 inch) thick. Crush garlic in base of an ovenproof dish and sprinkle with thyme.
- Place altnerating layers of courgettes and tomatoes in the ovenproof dish.
- Pour on olive oil and cook for 3 to 4 hours in an oven preheated to 120°C.

This is a very easy recipe and the result is very pleasant as a summer dish. It can be eaten hot or cold.

Ingredients

6 LONG COURGETTES (100 TO 150 G)
1 KG RIPE TOMATOES
1 CLOVE GARLIC
THYME, SALT, PEPPER, OLIVE OIL

Sautéed Courgettes with Marjoram

Courgettes are often said to be tasteless. The recipe below will give you an opportunity to amaze your friends.
It is quick to make and is an excellent accompaniment to meat and fish.

- Cut courgettes into sticks 3cm (just over 1 inch) long and 1 cm (1/2 inch) wide. Sauté in very hot olive oil until deep golden.
- Add finely chopped shallot, stir and add chopped marjoram.
- Drain in a colander to remove the fat and serve piping hot.

Serves 6

4 SMALL, FIRM COURGETTES
1 SHALLOT (FINELY CHOPPED)
15 G MARJORAM
OLIVE OIL, SALT, PEPPER

Aubergine and Tomato Roulade

- Finely slice aubergines lengthways. Sprinkle with salt and leave for a few hours to disgorge. Rinse in cold water, dry and fry in a deep-fat fryer (avoid over-cooking or they will be too dry). Drain on kitchen paper or a teatowel.
- Flavour dry chopped tomatoes with tarragon and check seasoning.
- Spread tomatoes thinly over aubergines and roll up. Lay in an ovenproof dish. Pour on some olive oil and heat through.

At home, we call this the "Provençal Menu".

Serves 6

5 LARGE AUBERGINES
500 G TOMATOES (SKINNED AND CHOPPED)
10 G TARRAGON
SALT, PEPPER, OLIVE OIL

Artichokes

There is no doubt that this is a Mediterranean vegetable. It is said to have originated in Sicily. Wherever it came from, our grateful thanks to Catherine de' Medici who introduced it into France. I shall only give you recipes for purple artichokes and poivrades, raw artichokes served with sea salt and olive oil.

STUFFED ARTICHOKES

Ingredients

12 PURPLE ARTICHOKES
2 CARROTS
2 ONIONS
1 WHOLE GARLIC
1 STICK CELERY
1 BUNCH BASIL
OLIVE OIL
THYME, BAY LEAF
STOCK

•Shape artichokes and retain white leaves. Dice carrots, onions and celery. Finely chop white artichoke leaves and stew gently with remainder of the vegetables. Fill artichoke hearts. Braise in stock with roughly chopped garlic, thyme and bay leaf. Simmer for 20 to 30 minutes depending on size. Remove hearts from pan and reduce stock. Add chopped basil and check seasoning.

GREEK-STYLE POIVRADE

Ingredients

18 SMALL ARTICHOKES
25 CL WHITE WINE
25 CL WATER
6 DSP. OLIVE OIL
1 LEMON (JUICE ONLY)
SALT, PEPPER, 10 CORIANDER SEEDS
1 BOUQUET GARNI (1 SPRIG THYME, 1 BAY LEAF, 1 STICK CELERY, ALL TIED TOGETHER)

•Prepare artichokes by cutting off stalks (leave only 2 cm (almost 1 inch)). Remove any hard leaves and cut tips of leaves.

•In a fairly large saucepan, bring to boil white wine, water, oil, salt, pepper, coriander, bouquet garni and lemon juice.

•When herb and wine mixture is boiling hard, add artichokes and cook over a high heat for 7 to 8 minutes but no more. The artichokes are very tender and they soon break up.

•Remove and place them stalk uppermost.

•Reduce liquor by half and pour into serving dish with artichokes. Leave to cool.

•Serve as an hors d'oeuvre, hot or cold. A superb dish!

ARTICHOKE FLAN

Ingredients

200 G PURPLE ARTICHOKE HEARTS
1 BAY LEAF
1 SPRIG ROSEMARY
7 EGGS
50 CL SINGLE CREAM

•Prepare artichokes and sprinkle on lemon juice if you are not ready to cook them immediately. Cook with a bay leaf and rosemary.

•Liquidise artichokes with three eggs and four yolks. Add cream and liquidise again. Strain through a Chinese sieve.

•Preheat the oven (Thermostat 5). Pour mixture into a cake tin or individual ramekins. Bake slowly in a bain-marie. By setting the eggs slowly, you can be sure of a perfect flan.

Stuffed Artichokes

Tomatoes à la provençale

There are umpteen thousand recipes for tomatoes à la provençale. Every mother and grandmother has her own. Every family and every household has its own. And everybody swears that theirs is the only authentic recipe and the best. Of course, everybody claims to be right!

Serves 4

8 LARGE, RIPE TOMATOES
50 G GARLIC
1 BOUQUET FLAT PARSLEY
150 G WHITE BREADCRUMBS
SALT, PEPPER
OLIVE OIL
THYME

My recipe

- Preheat the oven.
- Chop garlic and parsley.
- Cut tomatoes in half. Press them sharply to remove seeds.
- Lay tomatoes out on a baking tray or in a gratin dish. Season with salt and pepper and dust with thyme.
- Mix parsley and garlic with a little olive oil and the breadcrumbs to form a thick, fatty paste.
- Fill tomatoes with paste and cook for 20 to 30 minutes at 150 to 160°C.

I like my tomatoes well cooked but not dry, as some people prefer them. I like them to retain some of their juiciness. Tomatoes à la provençale can be eaten hot with a glass of well chilled rosé. It's a simple, convivial dish!

In order to avoid serious family arguments, I feel obliged to give you a recipe for the other way of preparing tomatoes à la provençale. Cooked in this second way, they add a delicious flavour to grilled meats or fish.

Generally speaking, they are eaten hot but some older locals like them, cold, on a crisp baguette with just a dribble of olive oil for breakfast.

To cook them properly, you must have a large, heavy-bottomed frying pan or two smaller pans.

- Cut tomatoes in half through the middle, and not from stem to base as certain tourists do.

• Remove seeds. Sprinkle salt on the halves. Lay tomatoes in a frying pan, salted side down, and add a few drops of oil. Begin cooking over a high heat. The "juice" will run from the tomatoes.

• Finely chop parsley and garlic with a knife or chopper.

• When the tomatoes have given off all their "juice" and it has evaporated, turn tomatoes over, season with pepper and sprinkle with a good pinch of parsley and garlic. Add a pinch of sugar, if liked. Lower heat and cook for as long as possible. The tomatoes will dry up but this is the aim of the exercise. It they stick to the pan, lower the heat as far as possible and add a small quantity of water. This creates a dark sauce in which the tomatoes caramelise.

• Keep a close watch on the tomatoes. They will dry up each time the sauce has evaporated and you will have to add a few drops of water. When there is nothing left but a small quantity of flesh, parsley and garlic in the wrinkled skin and when the sauce has caramelised for the last time and almost totally evaporated, the tomatoes are cooked.

• Serve with a few drops of raw olive oil.

Serves 4

8 TO 10 TOMATOES
2 CLOVES GARLIC (AT LEAST)
20 G FLAT PARSLEY
SALT, PEPPER
OLIVE OIL
1 PINCH SUGAR (OPTIONAL)

Tomatoes à la provençale

Chard with Cream and Anchovies

Chard

Chard is a traditional Christmas dish in Provence. It is a Mediterranean vegetable which still grows in the wild in Provence where it can reach heights of 1.50 to 2 metres (5 to 6 1/2 ft.). It is a member of the artichoke family and has the same flower.

We shall restrict ourselves to cultivated chard which come into season with the first frosts. Only the stems are edible, and they must be peeled first, which makes your fingers very black. The chard is then cut into small sticks and immediately put into water to which lemon juice has been added, to ensure that they do not blacken. Chard is always boiled first before being prepared.

CHARD WITH CREAM AND ANCHOVIES

●Prepare and cook chard as indicated above.

To obtain one kilo of chard, you will require one or two heads because there is a lot of waste.

●Melt the anchovy fillets in a fairly large saucepan with a little water, stirring continuously with a wooden spoon. When anchovies form a paste, add cream and bring to boil.

●Meanwhile, place chard in a gratin dish. When cream has reduced by half, check seasoning and pour over chard. Sprinkle grated cheese on top.

●Finish cooking for 15 to 20 minutes in the oven (160°C).

The gratin should be golden brown. This is an ideal dish with leg of lamb or roast chicken.

Serves 6 to 8

1 KG CHARD
1 LITRE CREAM
200 G SWISS CHEESE (GRATED)
6 ANCHOVY FILLETS
SALT, PEPPER, NUTMEG

COLD CARDOONS

Cardoons are excellent in salad.

●Choose the most tender stems from two cardoons for 8 people. Cut into pieces 6 to 7 cm (almost 3 inches) long and 2 to 3 cm (approximately 1 inch) wide. Cook in well salted water.

●Make an anchovy vinaigrette with 6 salted anchovy fillets soaked in water for several hours to remove salt.

●Melt in a saucepan, add two crushed cloves garlic, two spoons good vinegar and two spoons olive oil.

This makes a light anchovy vinaigrette in which to dip the cold cardoons.

Fennel

Fennel is a Mediterranean vegetable and, for many years, it was unknown outside the Nice area. Indeed, it was singularly unsuccessful in conquering the rest of the world. We, in Provence, consider it to be a superb vegetable which can be eaten raw, cooked, preserved etc. In short, it is the original all-purpose garnish.

It is excellent with meat and fish and can even be used to make a delicious dessert, preserved in sugar with a few spices.

BRAISED FENNEL WITH SAFFRON

Ingredients

6 FENNEL HEADS
2 ONIONS
THYME, BAY
1 CARROT
2 CLOVES GARLIC
25 CL WHITE WINE
1 G SAFFRON
SALT, PEPPER
OLIVE OIL

•Cut heads in half. Remove hard leaves (they can be used to make a cream or a soup). Blanch well in salted water and leave to cool.

•Meanwhile, finely dice onions and carrot (3 mm pieces). Crush garlic and sauté with onions and carrot in a small quantity of olive oil. The sauté pan should be large enough to take all the ingredients.

•When onions and carrots have sweated well, lay fennel on top. Ensure that none of the pieces touches another one. Add thyme and bay. Mix saffron into white wine and pour into sauté pan. Add water to cover vegetables. Bring to boil, season with salt and pepper.

•Cover and simmer gently in the oven (180°C) for 2 hours.

•When cooked, remove fennel. Reduce sauce then strain through a Chinese sieve and add some olive oil to emulsify.

This is wonderful with grilled fish or white meats.

ASPARAGUS TIP GRATIN

Serves 6

5 TO 8 ASPARAGUS TIPS (DEPENDING ON SIZE) PER PERSON
1 LITRE CHICKEN STOCK
1/2 LEMON
SALT, PEPPER, NUTMEG
2 EGGS
BUTTER, FLOUR

•Cook asparagus tips in salted water. Leave plenty of space between tips.

•Make a white sauce by using 70g flour and 80g butter to make a roux. Mix well without allowing to colour. Pour in chicken stock and cook for a fairly long time over a low heat. Season with salt, pepper and a little nutmeg. Add a few drops lemon juice.

•Carefully drain asparagus tips then lay in a gratin dish. Preheat oven to 100°C.

•Remove saucepan from heat and blend egg yolks into white sauce, whisking gently.

•Pour over asparagus tips until just covered and bake for 1 hour at 100°C.

•Ten minutes before serving, increase heat and place under the grill to brown the surface.

Braised Fennel with Saffron

Tomato, Aubergine and Mozzarella Slice

Serves 6

8 TOMATOES
4 AUBERGINES
200 G MOZZARELLA
GARLIC, SHALLOT
THYME, BAY
50 CL OLIVE OIL
PEPPER

• Slice aubergines into rounds and cook in olive oil until deep golden on both sides. Cut tomatoes into rounds and fry over a high heat. At the last moment, add chopped garlic and shallot, a few sprigs of thyme and powdered mace.

• Put alternating layers of aubergine and tomatoes in moulds. Bake in a hot oven (150°C) for 30 minutes.

• Moisten sauce slightly with olive oil. Cover with mozzarella cheese and brown under the grill.

This dish can be eaten on its own, as a hot hors d'oeuvre or even cold, with a vinaigrette. A good rosé or a light red are excellent as an accompaniment.

Tomato, Aubergine and Mozzarella Slice

Desserts

QUINCE TURNOVERS

Serves 4

- Make syrup with 1 litre water and sugar. Cook whole quince, with skin, in syrup. Leave in syrup to cool.
- Meanwhile, prepare 4 rounds of pastry 20 cm (8 inches) in diameter and 3 mm thick.
- Dice quince, removing pips but leaving skin.
- Spread compote in middle of pastry and top with diced quince.
- Fold pastry to make turnover and seal with egg yolk.
- Use remaining egg yolk to brush over pastry.
- Prick with fork and bake in an oven preheated to 180°C.
- Bake for 20 minutes.

I advise you to eat them while warm. They are tastier hot than cold.

4 RIPE QUINCE
PUFF PASTRY
4 SPOONS APPLE COMPOTE
1 EGG YOLK
SYRUP
1 LITRE WATER
750 G SUGAR

GREEN TOMATO TART

Serves 6

- Skin tomatoes and caramelise in syrup (1 kg sugar for 1 litre water). When syrup boils, add tomatoes, bring back to boil then leave to cool for several hours.
- Quarter tomatoes and remove seeds. Put tomatoes back in syrup with ground ginger and cloves. Bring back to boil and leave to cool.
- Use seeds to make a compote (cook again with a small quantity of syrup) to spread on precooked pastry base.
- Lay out tomatoes in concentric circles.

- Serve hot or cold with an apricot coulis.

8 GREEN TOMATOES
100 G SWEET SHORTCRUST PASTRY
14 G GROUND GINGER
3 CLOVES

FENNEL SORBET

Ingredients

900 G CASTOR SUGAR
12 G STABILISER
300 G DRIED FENNEL
2 LITRES WATER

- Place sugar, stabiliser, and dried fennel in a saucepan. Pour on 1 litre water and bring to boil.
- When mixture begins to boil, turn off heat and leave to infuse for approximately 30 minutes. Then add second litre of water.
- Leave until cold and mix.

Fennel Sorbet

PINE-KERNEL TART

- Mix butter, sugar and pinch of salt and beat until smooth and white. Gradually add egg yolks. Blend in flour. Beat as little as possible. Leave for 4 hours before using.
- Roll out pastry and line a sufficiently large tin for 8 people. Bake blind for a few minutes in a hot oven (200°C).
- Make a pale caramel with butter. Add pine-kernels.
- Cook then deglaze with cream.
- Put back over heat for a few minutes.
- Pour pine-kernel and cream mixture into pastry case.
- Bake for 20 minutes at 160°C.

Pine-Kernel Tart

Serves 8

PASTRY
125 G BUTTER
125 G SUGAR
4 EGG YOLKS
250 G FLOUR
SALT
1 VANILLA POD

FILLING
100 G SUGAR
100 G BUTTER
400 G PINE-KERNELS
25 CL DOUBLE CREAM

Roast Pears with Mulled Wine

Roast Pears with Mulled Wine

- Make the mulled wine: combine wine, orange juice, lemon slices, orange slices, sugar, anise flowers, cinnamon stick and cloves. Bring to boil and strain through a Chinese sieve.
- Peel pears and remove cores without breaking pears.
- Bring wine back to boil and add pears.
- Prick with a knife blade to check whether pears are cooked.
- Cool pears in wine to ensure that they take up the colour.

Serves 4

4 PEARS
1 LITRE RED WINE
25 CL ORANGE JUICE
1 LEMON (SLICED)
1 ORANGE (SLICED)
250 G SUGAR
3 ANISE FLOWERS
1 CINNAMON STICK
2 CLOVES

Caramelised Apples

- Peel apples and cut into eight. Remove pips.
- Make caramel with butter, honey and sugar. As soon as caramel begins to turn brown, add apples and sauté.
- When apples are well coated with caramel, cook gently for 3 to 4 minutes.
- Remove from pan and lay on a serving dish.
- Deglaze remaining caramel with apple brandy, after removing pan from heat. The sauce should be a warm golden colour. Drizzle round the apples.

Serves 6

1 KG APPLES (Golden Delicious or Cox's)
1 BOTTLE CIDER
1/2 GLASS APPLE BRANDY ("Calvados")
200 G SUGAR
200 G HONEY
100 G BUTTER

Darphin Apples

- Peel and grate apple. Sprinkle with sugar while grating and, if necessary, add few drops of lemon juice to prevent apple from discolouring. Add cognac and mix well.
- Beat eggs and blend into apple mixture. Cook like an omelette with a small knob of butter. Turn omelette over and cook other side.

Ingredients for 1 person

1 APPLE
2 EGGS
CASTOR SUGAR
FEW DROPS LEMON JUICE
3 CL COGNAC

RED FRUITS IN SYRUP

Ingredients

20 G GRAND MARNIER
250 G CASTOR SUGAR
500 G WATER
50 G RASPBERRIES
50 G WILD STRAWBERRIES
50 G REDCURRANTS
50 G BLACKBERRIES (BRAMBLES)
50 G BLACKCURRANTS

•Place sugar in a saucepan and add water. Bring to boil and cool. When syrup is cold, pour over fruit and stir gently to avoid squashing fruit.

LEMON AND BASIL SORBET

Ingredients

1.25 LITRES WATER
450 G SUGAR
300 G LEMON JUICE
1/2 BUNCH BASIL

This is a simple recipe and it is very refreshing in hot weather.

•Mix water, sugar, lemon juice and basil.

•Bring to boil then strain through a fine-meshed Chinese sieve. Put in deep freeze and as soon as it begins to "take", scrape with a fork.

HONEY-BRAISED PEACHES WITH LAVENDER ICE CREAM

Serves 4

600 G PEACHES (QUARTERED)
1 DSP. LAVENDER HONEY

Ice Cream

50 CL MILK
6 EGG YOLKS
125 G SUGAR
NATURAL LAVENDER FLAVOURING
(QUANTITY IS A MATTER OF PERSONAL CHOICE)

•Make lavender ice cream.

•Braise peaches in a frying pan with butter and honey.

•Lay peach quarters round edge of plate.

•Pour warm honey remaining in frying pan over peaches.

•Place a scoop of lavender ice cream in the centre of the plate.

PROVENÇAL SHUTTLES

Ingredients

750 G FLOUR
375 G CASTOR SUGAR
65 G BUTTER
3 EGGS
10 CL WATER
1 LEMON (ZEST ONLY)
SALT

•Make a fountain with flour and place sugar, softened butter, zests, a pinch of salt, and eggs in centre. Blend in water to obtain a smooth paste.

•Make sausage shapes of the size preferred. Cut into sections and pat into an oval shape.

•Lay on a greased baking sheet. Slash centre of each shuttle and leave for 1 hour. Brush with egg yolk.

•Bake at a moderate temperature and remove from oven when shuttles are golden brown.

Red Fruits in Syrup

HAZELNUT BRITTLE

Ingredients

500 G CASTOR SUGAR
100 G EGG WHITES
200 G WHOLE HAZELNUTS
50 G FLOUR

- Mix sugar and flour. Then add egg whites and stir to produce a fairly liquid paste.
- Lastly, add whole hazelnuts and shape small balls with a diameter of approximately 2 cm (almost 1 inch).
- Lay on a baking tray covered with greaseproof paper and bake for 5 minutes at 180°C.

Hazelnut Brittle

LETTUCE AND RHUBARB TART

- Roll pastry out 2 mm thick to line a tin.
- Roll up 12 small balls of rhubarb and wrap in lettuce leaves, rolling them up as if you were making beef olives.
- Lay out on the pastry.
- Pour over custard.
- Bake in an oven preheated to 150°C for 15 to 20 minutes.

Serves 6

12 LARGE LETTUCE LEAVES (WELL BLANCHED)
300 G RHUBARB (ROUGHLY CUT INTO STICKS, BLANCHED, SAUTÉED IN A FRYING PAN TO COLOUR THEN SPRINKLED WITH SUGAR)
PUFF PASTRY

Custard filling

2 EGG YOLKS
1 WHOLE EGG
100 G SUGAR
2 VANILLA PODS
50 CL SINGLE CREAM

Preserved Grapefruit

PRESERVED GRAPEFRUIT

- Peel grapefruit and blanch in water.
- Bring sugar and water to boil. As soon as syrup is boiling, add pieces of grapefruit and leave to caramelise for a whole day over a very low heat.
- When grapefruit is cooked, it is transparent. Leave to cool in syrup then drain for half-a-day on a grid.
- Cut into 0.5 cm (1/4 inch) slices and dip in sugar.

Ingredients

4 GRAPEFRUIT
1 KG CASTOR SUGAR
1.5 LITRES WATER

Nut-Stuffed Tomatoes

Serves 4

4 TOMATOES
300 G CASTOR SUGAR
50 G WALNUT KERNELS
50 G SLICED ALMONDS
50 G HAZELNUTS
50 G PINE KERNELS
150 G SINGLE CREAM

- Skin tomatoes: put in boiling water and leave for approximately 20 seconds. Remove from water and cool immediately in iced water. They are then easy to skin.
- Cut off a "hat" and empty out flesh, removing seeds and remainder of flesh.
- Make a caramel: cook sugar in a saucepan, with no added water. Cook until caramel is a good dark brown.
- Add single cream and mix. Turn off heat and add dried fruit.
- Garnish tomatoes with nut and caramel mixture and replace the "hat".

Ingredients

4 EGG YOLKS
150 G SUGAR AT 121 °C
185 BUTTER (MELTED)
100 G DARK CHOCOLATE (COUVERTURE CHOCOLATE, MELTED)
60 G TRUFFLES
350 G WHIPPED CREAM

Chocolate Truffles

- Beat egg yolks and sugar then blend in melted butter and chocolate. Leave until cold.
- Blend in whipped cream and grated truffles.

Serves 4 to 6

6 EGG YOLKS
100 G CASTOR SUGAR
250 G SINGLE CREAM
100 G MILK
1 G DRIED
LAVENDER
FLOWERS

Lavender-Flavoured Creme Brûlée

- Mix egg yolks with sugar, whisking swiftly until white.
- Add cream, cold milk and lavender.
- Leave mixture to rest for 1 or 2 hours to pick up full flavour of the lavender.
- Pour into an egg dish or ovenproof pottery plate.
- Bake at 130°C in a bain-marie for 1 1/4 hours.
- Remove from oven and allow to cool.

It is advisable to make this dish in the morning for the evening meal.

Nut-Stuffed Tomatoes

The Thirteen Desserts

In Provence, the Christmas festivities begin very simply with a meal served early enough on Christmas Eve to enable guests to finish it in time for Midnight Mass.

In memory of the seven sacred wounds of Christ, seven dishes are placed on the table, each containing the following three ingredients:

- garlic and sage, plants which are reputed to have miraculous virtues;
- a non-oily fish.

To complete this humble meal, thirteen desserts are served. This may appear to be "over the top" but they are actually very modest offerings - dates, walnuts, hazelnuts, figs, sultanas, almonds, dark nougat, white nougat, mandarine oranges, citrus rectangles, oreillettes, quince jujube and fougasse.

Dates: A blessed fruit because a date palm provided the Virgin Mary with shelter during the Flight into Egypt.

Dried fruit: Walnuts, hazelnuts, figs, sultanas and almonds are all reminders of the richness of the region and all are part of the summer harvest stored for the winter months.

Nougat: Dark nougat is very hard; white nougat is softer.

Mandarine oranges: A much-appreciated fruit whose skin, if thrown onto the fire, gives off a wonderful aroma.

Citrus rectangles: The outer "shell" of this sweetmeat conceals a surprise that delights children.

Oreillettes and quince jujube: They can be home-made. Indeed, it is traditional for families to make up the thirteen desserts?

Fougasse: This is one of the gifts laid before the actors in the Nativity play performed during the Midnight Mass.

Truffle Ice-Cream

TRUFFLE ICE-CREAM

- Put an empty mixing bowl in the refrigerator. Meanwhile, boil up the milk with the vanilla pod.

- Make a custard by beating 250 g sugar with egg yolks. Pour on milk and simmer gently. The custard is ready when it coats the spoon. Remove vanilla pod and leave to cool.

- Whip the cream with 50 g sugar until stiff in the cool mixing bowl.

- When custard has cooled, gently blend in whipped cream and finely chopped truffles.

- Fill one or more moulds and place in deep freeze.

Ingredients

8 EGG YOLKS
250 + 50 G SUGAR
1/2 VANILLA POD
1/2 LITRE MILK
1 POT FRESH CREAM
20 G TRUFFLES

CITRUS RECTANGLES

Ingredients

1 KG FLOUR
40 G SUGAR
3 ORANGES (GRATED)
2 LEMONS (GRATED)
10 G GROUND NUT OIL
1/2 ORANGE (JUICE ONLY)
125 G MELTED SUGAR
3 EGGS
ICING SUGAR

- Knead flour, sugar, eggs, orange juice, lemon and orange zests to obtain a smooth paste. Mix in melted butter.
- Roll out fairly thinly. Cut out rectangles and fry in very hot oil then drain on kitchen paper.
- Once cooked and drained, dust with icing sugar.

QUINCE JUJUBE

- Select ripe quince. Wash and quarter, with skin and pips.
- Place in a saucepan, barely cover with water and cook.
- When soft, drain and strain through a Moulinette.
- Weigh the puree and use 1 kg sugar to 1 kg puree.
- Place in a preserving pan and cook gently, stirring all the time.
- Ask somebody to help you with this recipe. It takes at least half-an-hour and your arm will tire quickly as you move the wooden spoon continuously back and forward through the mixture.
- To test whether the quince jujube is cooked, pour a small quantity onto a plate. If it remains compact, it is ready. Pour mixture onto a baking tray and leave to cool.
- Cut into pieces.

POMPE À L'HUILE OR FOUGASSE

This is the Provençal recipe *par excellence*. It is a vital part of traditional Christmas celebrations.

Ingredients

125 G AND 325 G FLOUR
150 G SUGAR
10 CL OLIVE OIL
1 ORANGE
1 LEMON
20 G BAKER'S YEAST
1 EGG YOLK
2 DSP. ORANGE FLOWER WATER

- On previous day, prepare a leaven with 125 g flour, baker's yeast and 8 cl water.
- Leave to rise overnight.
- The next day, grate zests of orange and lemon. Place 325 g flour in a mixing bowl and make a well in the centre. Add sugar, salt, oil and orange flower water. Mix with leaven to obtain a smooth dough. Leave to rise for 30 minutes.

Citrus Rectangles

- Beat dough on the working surface to remove all fermenting gases.
- Roll out to 1 cm (1/2 inch) thick. Cut out rectangles and slash in middle with a knife.
- Bake in an oven preheated to 180°C for 20 minutes.

White Nougat

Ingredients

700 G HONEY
175 G EGG WHITES, HEATED AND BEATEN UNTIL STIFF
400 G GLUCOSE
800 G SUGAR
300 G WATER
900 G WHOLE ROAST ALMONDS

- Pour cooked sugar (glucose + sugar + water cooked at 140°C) and honey over stiffly-beaten egg whites. Leave until cold.
- Add hot almonds. Pour immediately onto a well-greased baking tray and leave until cold.
- Cut pieces of the required size.

Dark nougat

Ingredients

500 G HONEY
50 G GLUCOSE
500 G GRILLED ALMONDS IN THEIR SKINS

- Heat honey in a saucepan with glucose until caramelised.
- Add hot grilled almonds and stir with a wooden spoon.
- Pour nougat onto greaseproof paper and leave to cool for a few hours.
- Cut nougat to required size with a serrated knife.

Dark nougat

Table of Contents

Front cover:
Photo: Eric Cattin

Cet ouvrage a été achevé d'imprimer en France par l'imprimerie Mame à Tours (37)
I.S.B.N. 2.7373.2502.1 - N° d'éditeur : 3890.03.1,5.02.05
Dépôt légal : avril 1999

MAME